Celtic Christian Spirituality

Selected Books in the
SkyLight Illuminations Series

The Art of War—Spirituality for Conflict: Annotated & Explained

Bhagavad Gita: Annotated & Explained

*The Book of Common Prayer: A Spiritual Treasure Chest—
Selections Annotated & Explained*

The Book of Mormon: Selections Annotated & Explained

Celtic Christian Spirituality: Essential Writings—Annotated & Explained

*Desert Fathers and Mothers: Early Christian Wisdom Sayings—
Annotated & Explained*

*The Divine Feminine in Biblical Wisdom Literature: Selections Annotated &
Explained*

Ecclesiastes: Annotated & Explained

*Embracing the Divine Feminine: Finding God through the Ecstasy of
Physical Love—The Song of Songs Annotated & Explained*

The Gospel of Thomas: Annotated & Explained

Hasidic Tales: Annotated & Explained

The Hebrew Prophets: Selections Annotated & Explained

*John and Charles Wesley: Selections from Their Writings and Hymns—
Annotated & Explained*

*Julian of Norwich: Selections from Revelations of Divine Love—
Annotated & Explained*

The Meditations of Marcus Aurelius: Selections Annotated & Explained

Native American Stories of the Sacred: Annotated & Explained

*Perennial Wisdom for the Spiritually Independent: Sacred Teachings—
Annotated & Explained*

Philokalia: The Eastern Christian Spiritual Texts—Annotated & Explained

Proverbs: Annotated & Explained

*The Qur'an and Sayings of Prophet Muhammad: Selections Annotated &
Explained*

*Rumi and Islam: Selections from His Stories, Poems, and Discourses—
Annotated & Explained*

The Sacred Writings of Paul: Selections Annotated & Explained

*Saint Augustine of Hippo: Selections from Confessions and Other Essential
Writings—Annotated & Explained*

*Saint Ignatius Loyola—The Spiritual Writings: Selections Annotated &
Explained*

Spiritual Writings on Mary: Annotated & Explained

Tao Te Ching: Annotated & Explained

The Way of a Pilgrim: The Jesus Prayer Journey—Annotated & Explained

Zohar: Annotated & Explained

Celtic Christian Spirituality

Essential Writings— Annotated and Explained

Annotation by Mary C. Earle

Foreword by John Philip Newell

Walking Together, Finding the Way ®
SKYLIGHT PATHS ®
PUBLISHING
Nashville, Tennessee

Celtic Christian Spirituality:
Essential Writings—Annotated and Explained

2015 Quality Paperback Edition

Library of Congress Cataloging-in-Publication Data
Celtic Christian spirituality : essential writings / annotated and explained, Mary C. Earle ; foreword by John Philip Newell. — Quality paperback ed.
    p. cm. — (SkyLight illuminations)
  Includes bibliographical references.
  ISBN 978-1-59473-302-4 (quality pbk.)
  ISBN 978-1-68336-007-0 (hardcover)
  1. Spirituality—Celtic Church. 2. Celtic Church—Doctrines. I. Earle, Mary C.
  BR748.C36 2011
  248.3'20923916—dc22
                                                                2011014397

ISBN 978-1-59473-319-2 (eBook)

Cover Design: Walter C. Bumford III, Stockton, Massachusetts
Cover Art: "Celtic Cross on Cornish Church" © iStockphoto.com/Chris Leather
Manufactured in the United States of America

SkyLight Paths Publishing is creating a place where people of different spiritual traditions come together for challenge and inspiration, a place where we can help each other understand the mystery that lies at the heart of our existence.

SkyLight Paths sees both believers and seekers as a community that increasingly transcends traditional boundaries of religion and denomination—people wanting to learn from each other, *walking together, finding the way.*

SkyLight Paths, "Walking Together, Finding the Way" and colophon are trademarks of LongHill Partners, Inc., registered in the U.S. Patent and Trademark Office.

Walking Together, Finding the Way®
Published by SkyLight Paths Publishing
An imprint of Turner Publishing Company
4507 Charlotte Avenue, Suite 100
Nashville, TN 37209
Tel: (615) 255-2665
www.skylightpaths.com

For my teachers, especially Dr. V. Nelle Bellamy (1922–2009)
and the Rev. Dr. William B. Green (1927–2011)

Contents ☐

Foreword   ix

Acknowledgments   xi

Introduction   1

1. Creation   19

2. Prayer   49

3. Incarnation   69

4. Daily Life and Work   81

5. Soul Friends   103

6. Pilgrimage   109

7. Social Justice   117

8. Blessing as a Way of Life   133

Notes   140

Suggestions for Further Reading   141

Credits   143

Foreword □

A *foreword* is a word before other words. It is a word that prepares the way. If I were to offer one word to prepare the way for the many beautiful words of Mary Earle's *Celtic Christian Spirituality*, it would be "grace-filled." Her words bring to life the essential wisdom of these Celtic texts. Or perhaps the word should be "illuminating," for she throws light on forgotten truths. Or yet again maybe the word should be "heartfelt," for she speaks from her heart as well as from the fine clarity of her mind. So you see, I need to say more than one thing about Mary Earle's offering, for she has brought many gifts to this collection.

First, she keeps reminding us of the essential oneness of life. In the Celtic Christian world, heaven and earth are not divided. Spirit and matter are woven together inseparably. The life of one species and the life of another are never torn apart. The well-being of humanity is viewed in relationship to the well-being of the rest of earth's species. And the health of the individual is not severed from the health of the community. The one and the many belong together. The microcosm and the macrocosm are one. Time and eternity are wedded. Carl Jung, the founder of analytical psychology, says that the devil is a dualist. The devil is forever trying to rip apart what God has joined together. Mary Earle's selections and commentary are an antidote to the dualisms that are dangerously dividing us. She keeps pointing to Celtic Christianity's gift for today, its vision of interbeing.

Second, she does not forget the brokenness of life, the wounds that are deep in the human soul, and the agonies of earth's body and species. To speak of humanity as made in the image of God, and to include texts that point to creation as theophany, is not to slip into naive romanticism.

Anyone who knows Mary Earle's journey knows that the deepest pains of life's struggle and sorrow are not foreign to her. She brings to this work the integrity of holding together a vision of life's sacredness with a full consciousness of life's woundedness. The fourteenth-century mystic Julian of Norwich sees in one of her dreamlike awarenesses of Jesus that he is very handsome because in his countenance there is both joy and sorrow. It is this combination that Mary Earle beautifully brings to her writing.

And third, she never strays far from practice—the practice of prayer, the practice of soul-friending, the practice of pilgrimage, the practice of social justice. Transformation will happen in our lives and world only through practice and practice and practice. This is an essential feature of Celtic Christianity, as it is of any great spiritual tradition. Mary Earle knows this and keeps drawing our attention to the priority of embodied practice. Yes, we must remember the essential oneness and sacredness of everything that has being. Yes, we must look at brokenness straight in the face in our lives and the world. But, if we are to be part of change and healing, we must also find practices that strengthen the deepest yearnings of our being for wholeness. The twelfth-century teacher Hildegard of Bingen speaks of the kiss of choice. Practice is about choosing to be strong for the way of love. Mary Earle casts fresh light on a tradition that is brimful with practice. Her offering is grace-filled, illuminating, heartfelt. It is a blessing.

John Philip Newell

Acknowledgments ☐

Over the years, I have benefited from the teaching and counsel of a variety of scholars who study these texts. I am especially grateful for the kind support of Saunders and Cynthia Davies, John Philip Newell, the late John O'Donohue, Patrick Thomas, Esther de Waal, and the late A. M. Allchin. They have been friends along the way, and have encouraged my own study and prayer. I am grateful to Sister Cintra Pemberton of the Order of Saint Helena of the Episcopal Church for my time with her on pilgrimage to Ireland and Wales.

My editors, Nancy Fitzgerald, Emily Wichland, and Lauren Hill, have answered countless questions and been patient and clear in their responses.

As ever, I am grateful to Doug, my husband, who served as first reader and steady encourager.

Lastly, I give thanks for all my students over the years. Their questions and conversation have enriched my life, focused my study, deepened my prayer, widened my learning. To each of you, thanks. For each of you, thanks.

Introduction ☐

Some twenty-five years ago, when I was finishing up my seminary training and wondering what had happened to my prayer life, one of my men-
tors, Dr. V. Nelle Bellamy, returned from a trip to England with a gift book
for me. Titled *Celtic Prayers* and embellished with illustrations inspired by
The Book of Kells, an illuminated book of gospels, this little text opened
a door for me. While reading that book, and praying those prayers, I went
through a spiritual portal into a way of prayer, a way of seeing, a way of
practicing the Christian faith. As I voiced the prayers in that volume,
prayers from the Hebrides written down in the late nineteenth century, I
found that something within me awakened, stirred, began to grow
stronger. The aridity that too much speculative theology and doctrinal
wrangling had created within me began to dissipate. A sense of faith, living and true, strong and robust, playful and forthright, came through
those prayers. I had begun to explore the expression of Christian life and
faith found in the Celtic cultures.

Two years later, on the occasion of my ordination to the priesthood
in the Episcopal Church, Dr. Bellamy gave me another small book. This
one was an anthology of prayers from the lands we know as "Celtic"—
Scotland, Ireland, Wales, Brittany, Cornwall, the Isle of Man, and Galicia in
Spain. *Threshold of Light*, edited by A. M. Allchin and Esther de Waal,
offered a thirty-day rota of prayer for the morning and the evening.[1] The
first year of my priestly life, I prayed those prayers daily. They are intrin-
sically woven into my life as wife, mother, priest, writer, spiritual director,
teacher, and retreat leader. Lines from those prayers find their way into
conversation, reflection, e-mails, sermons, and journals. They were the
first threads of a larger fabric woven within me by reading and studying

the expressions of Christian life and faith found in these lands. These threads are also woven through the gospels and the life of the early Christian church. In this introduction, I invite you to begin reflecting on these themes and the ways in which they enrich the Christian way.

My hope is that you will discover a spiritual path that intentionally encourages attention and care for all of creation. In our present ecological dilemmas, so fraught with anxiety and fear, the Celtic way of seeing God's presence in and through all matter changes our perspective. We are invited to let go of anxiety and to embrace wonder. We find ourselves challenged to handle the creation with a growing awareness of its Source. We discover that no people, no nation, no religion has the final say on distribution of resources and goods, for an infinitely gracious God desires that we emulate God's own generosity. We remember that personal practice and public policy are connected. We seek ways to honor and to respect the sacred Presence that dwells within all matter and in whom we all live. The links between contemplative prayer and compassionate action become clearer. Our minds and our hearts begin to work together for the good of all bodies, whether they be the bodies of humans, creatures, or the Earth itself.

In short, this is a tradition that recalls the radical nature of the message of Jesus. Learning to love God, our neighbor, and ourselves is a life-long journey in which our awareness of the ways in which we are knit together calls the status quo into question. Whether through the lyrical poetry of Wales, the songs of the Hebridean people of Scotland, or Irish devotional poetry, this tradition wakes us up from our complacency, stirs our creativity, and calls us to steadfast practices of faith, hope, and love.

In this volume, I offer you many of the primary texts that have shaped my own life and prayer. They are also the texts that my students have found the most stirring and the most challenging over the twenty-plus years that I've taught this material. In other words, these are texts that have met these criteria: 1) The texts illustrate some aspect of the

Celtic Christian tradition; 2) The texts provoke reflection and prayer; and 3) The texts lead to deepening desire for personal and communal transformation.

Sources and Their Context

In some ways the word "Celtic" is misleading. It leads us to assume that the traditions found in Ireland, Scotland, Wales, Cornwall, Brittany, the Isle of Man, and Galicia are uniform. In fact, each country does have its own emphasis. The word "Celtic" is a linguistic term; it signals languages in a particular grouping. For our purposes, "Celtic" signifies both the areas where Celtic languages were and are spoken and the culturally formed spiritualities, historical and contemporary, that are linked to those languages. It is derived from the Greek word *keltoi*, which was used to name the peoples who lived on the fringes of Europe in ancient times.

In the texts that follow, there are selections from Wales, Ireland, and Scotland. Each of these traditions has its own distinct characteristics. Wales, for instance, had a flourishing of court poets and bards in the Middle Ages. Kings and queens sought talented bards who composed beautiful songs of praise, both for the royalty and for God. Some say that in the Welsh tradition it is impossible to pray without also speaking poetry. To this day, the tradition of poetry is alive and flourishing in Wales. Poets such as Ruth Bidgood, Saunders Lewis, R. S. Thomas, Euros Bowen, Waldo Williams, and Bobi Jones demonstrate the vitality and insight of the Celtic Christian spiritual tradition in contemporary contexts. From Ireland we receive prayers and poems marked by lyric qualities, both in the texts from the monastic and hermitic traditions and in the texts from oral tradition. From the Outer Hebrides of Scotland, a robust oral tradition has gifted us with songs and prayers that reflect an intimate awareness of God's presence in every moment and in every aspect of life. This lively Scottish tradition continues in the present day through the liturgies, hymns and prayers published by the Iona Community, a contemporary community of men and women who live a rule of life on the Hebridean island of Iona.

Saint Patrick of Ireland

I have included excerpts from the writings of Saint Patrick, from whom we have received two works, his *Confession* and his *Letter to Coroticus.* Patrick lived in the fifth century and was probably born on the west coast of Britain (though some now say that possibly he was born in Brittany). As a teenager, he was kidnapped by Irish slavers. From a Christian family, Patrick tells us that in the isolation of his time tending the sheep, exposed to the elements and under scrutiny by his master, he prayed with the aid of the Holy Spirit. After receiving a dream in which he was told to seek a ship that would take him to freedom, he set forth, walking all the way to the east coast of Ireland. A ship was in the harbor, and he was allowed to board. His life as a slave was over, but he never forgot being held against his will and living without the freedom he had taken for granted. As a result, his mature theology denounces any attempt to own or destroy another human being. Saint Patrick's voice sounds rather like a liberation theologian's. He is confident that the work of God within us and within society is exemplified by increasing freedom to choose to honor the dignity of every human being. Given his history, Patrick knew in his body and soul the denigration of slavery. His voice is one of the strongest we know in this regard from this early period of church history.

Pelagius

The selections from the writings of Pelagius, who probably came from what is now Wales, were penned in the late fourth and early fifth centuries. For most of Christian history, Pelagius has been regarded as a heretic, because we know of him primarily through the writings of Augustine of Hippo (354–430 CE). As Christian theologians asked the question, Why did God become human in Jesus? a variety of responses were offered. One answer maintained that humans had become so permanently and absolutely marred by "original sin" that we no longer bore the image and likeness of God. We humans were incapable of acting justly because our sin had eradicated the image of God within us. The argument follows that God became human in Jesus to offer atonement for sin on the cross. Augustine's writings clearly expressed despair in the human condition and articulated what became the doctrine of original sin. The corruption of original sin is, according to Augustine, passed from mother to child in the womb. (It is worth remembering that Augustine was writing as the Roman Empire experienced successive invasions from the north of Europe. He witnessed the conquering of an empire that had been the agent of cohesion in the ancient world. In some ways it is not surprising that his own views of humanity are so acutely despairing of the possibility of God-given goodness within the human community.)

Pelagius and his followers, on the other hand, clearly believed that God became human in Jesus to show us what being truly human would look like *and* to declare that the image of God could never be completely eradicated, because God is the one who fashions humanity in God's image. According to Pelagius, we cannot undo that essential dimension of human identity; the image of God within us is indestructible. We are creatures, and we cannot utterly destroy God's essential goodness in bringing forth life and sustaining that life. God continues to make humanity in God's image and likeness. God's grace and mercy are offered at every moment to aid us in growing more capable of reflecting the gracious life of the God who breathes us into being.

This ongoing disagreement over God's purpose in becoming human in Jesus is found throughout church history. It reflects the different ways of regarding God, human life, free will, salvation, and sin. One way in which the argument between Pelagius and Augustine was focused was in the polemic regarding baptism. Augustine maintained that a baby who died without benefit of baptism would not enter heaven. Pelagius adamantly refuted that premise, stating that a baby bears the image of God, and would of course be welcomed by God in eternity.

Upon visiting Rome, and discovering a church that was far too opulent for his ascetical spirit, Pelagius continued to insist on the radical nature of Jesus' life and ministry. Care for the poor; right distribution of wealth;

attention to the sick, the hungry, and those in prison; and kindness to the marginalized were the core of his vision and ministry. In some ways, Pelagius sounds like the prophet Amos of the Hebrew Scriptures. His writing no doubt made others uncomfortable. And his message troubled the ecclesial waters in Rome.

Pelagius was excommunicated and exiled by Pope Zosimus in 418. For centuries, he was known as a heretic. Only when his writings were translated into English, and when scholars began to read what he had actually written, were we able to hear his ongoing proclamation. Pelagius understands that the whole creation is in and of God, and that God infinitely transcends that creation. Because all matter has a divine origin, we have a sacred duty to care for the earth and for one another, and to share equitably the gifts we have been given.

As a native Celt, Pelagius lived in a culture in which women had the right to own property, divorce, study Latin and Greek (which generally was not the case in Europe), and become lawyers and physicians. He taught women with the expectation that they would become equal partners in the spreading of the gospel. Some of the selections of his writings in this volume come from his *Letters.* In those letters, we discover Pelagius's ability to articulate a scandalously vibrant sense of the Incarnation— scandalous because of the profound sense that matter and spirit are inherently compatible, and vibrant in the implications of that for Christian life and practice. It is even more scandalous because he teaches Demetrias, a young woman seeking spiritual counsel, and others this gospel of Jesus that offers full participation and inclusion to women!

John Scotus Eriugena

A ninth-century Irish teacher, Eriugena offers us theology that is both deeply influenced by the early theologians of the Christian east and true to his Irish roots. He spent time in the court of Charles the Bald, who ruled much of what is now France and also became the Holy Roman Emperor. Significantly, Eriugena translated the works of both Dionysius the Areopagite (late fifth to early sixth century)[2] and Maximus the Confessor (seventh century)[3] from Greek into Latin. The writings of these two theologians from the Christian east are mystical theologies. In different ways, each of them explores the mystery of the Incarnation.

Dionysius explicated the process of *theosis*: being made in the image and likeness of God, and by our own God-given capacity and the generous, ineffable working of God's grace, humans are transformed steadily into the likeness of God. Dionysius likens this to the process that a sculptor uses—that which is extraneous, which obscures or clutters the essential image hidden in marble, is slowly chipped away by the sculptor. In time, the true image that has been hidden from view is revealed. Something analogous transpires through theosis. We humans participate in the divine energies (not the essence of God, which is beyond our capacity to know or encounter). As we are bathed in the light of these divine energies (like sunlight is to the sun) we are transformed, body, mind, and spirit. (The Christian East has maintained that humanity may participate in the energies, or divine Light, emanating from the infinite God. We cannot, however, ever know God in God's self, for we are finite.) We become the person God intends us to become, humbly assenting to the workings of the Holy Spirit's transforming love within us. This is a deepening journey both into the life of God as Trinity and into the singular personhood that God creates for each of us. Even more astounding, our growth in the likeness of God is a process of divinization. We become Godlike, and our bodies, minds, and spirits are changed by the profound and inexhaustible workings of grace. We become radiant, shining with the glory that is God's own Light.

Maximus the Confessor observed that humans are both "microcosm and mediator." We stand between the worlds of heaven and earth, and yet the two are conjoined within us. Each of us is a little *kosmos*—a little universe in which God dwells. Because of our distinctively human place in the vast design of creation, we have a God-given vocation as mediators. We praise and adore God, and lead the whole earth in singing "Glory to you, God on high." In Jesus, through the power of the Holy Spirit, we intercede for all people, countries, creatures, places. In Jesus' humanity, because of the Incarnation, we see the high vocation to which we are called. The image of God, never lost, never eradicated, is intensified, magnified, made ever more true as we are made new through repentance and sorrow for forgetting our divine origin and destiny.

To this day, Jews and Eastern Orthodox Christians do not have a doctrine of original sin. Eastern Orthodox churches maintain that through the stunning gift of theosis, the Holy Spirit working in us to change us into truly Godlike creatures, we grow ever more fully into the likeness of God. Body, mind, and spirit participate ever more deeply in the uncreated Light that is God's. That participation changes us, makes us more capable of divine compassion. We befriend one another and the earth, and we truly practice learning to love our enemies.

This is a theological anthropology virtually unknown in the Christian west, except in the Celtic theologians and in mystical writers (see, for example, *Showings of Divine Love* by Julian of Norwich).[4] John Scotus Eriugena, in translating the works of Dionysius and Maximus, integrated their theological arguments into his native Irish theology and practice. Consequently, Eriugena offers us a theology that remembers that everything is one in Christ, because "without him not one thing came into being" (John 1:3). That oneness *is.* It is not our task to create the oneness. God in Christ, through the Holy Spirit, is the author of the oneness.

Our task is to perceive the Light in which all exists, and to live from that perception. When our sight is cleared by tears of sorrow for our forgetfulness, our blindness, our hurt of ourselves and one another, our greed, and our violence, we behold the universe as a sacred whole. As a consequence, our moral life is rooted and grounded in love—not romantic, sappy love, but the love that has brought the whole universe into being. Our moral life is not separate from our prayer life. They are, in fact, of a piece. In the deep silence of resting in God's presence and receiving the love that welcomes us, our God-given will to become like the Holy One grows ever stronger and more courageous.

Eriugena's terminology and form of expression may seem strange at first pass. However, he articulates a way of Christian life and practice that is influenced by the strong monastic life of Ireland, Wales, and Scotland. He applies the mystical insights from his own traditions and the mystical theology of Dionysius the Areopagite and Maximus the Confessor to how we live, how we treat one another, and how political and economic life is structured. From the point of view of Eriugena, when we hurt another person, when we engage in war, when we refuse to honor the common good, we are desecrating the very life of God, present and vital within all that God has spoken into being. This high theological anthropology, which calls us to a life of courageous compassion and hearty generosity, takes sins of omission and commission most seriously. Given this high calling, our failure to respond is a failure of deepest woe. Nevertheless, God is ever present, ready to forgive, heal, and make us whole and strong. God desires for us to grow ever more steadily into the image and likeness of the Holy One who breathes us into being.

The Carmina Gadelica

Prayers from *The Carmina Gadelica*, a six-volume collection of poems, hymns, charms, songs, and incantations compiled by Andrew Carmichael around the end of the nineteenth century, are strongly represented in this collection of texts. A Gaelic speaker and tax collector posted to various islands of the Outer Hebrides, Carmichael began collecting folklore and prayers from the native peoples of those islands. These prayers existed as oral tradition; Carmichael had to seek permission from the farmers, weavers, crofters, and fishermen to transcribe the originals in Gaelic. He then translated them into English. Though not a scholar, he took great care in recording the oral tradition and eventually published his findings.

The Carmina Gadelica reveals much to us about faith that is lived and practiced. It also continues to inform modern writers of prayer and liturgy, such as John Philip Newell and authors in the Iona Community. As is the case with any oral tradition, these prayers may indeed preserve a centuries-long tradition of prayer, perhaps giving us a sense of the prayer life that existed in that part of what is now Scotland during the Age of the Saints in the early Middle Ages.

George MacLeod and the Iona Community

George MacLeod, a Scot who was also a Presbyterian minister from a wealthy family, founded the contemporary Iona Community in 1938. Lord MacLeod became a captain in the British military service during World War I. His experience of the devastating trench warfare led to theological reflection. On a train with wounded soldiers returning home, he had a profound experience of Christ's presence in each of those shattered, shaken bodies. Out of that moment came a resolve to engage the disenfranchised and the poor. His life and ministry model a faithful dedication to the radical gospel that Pelagius saw so clearly. Lord MacLeod was known for striding the streets of Glasgow, asking people, "Are you making peace today?" Having witnessed firsthand the effects of war, he sought to find ways to address its underlying economic, social, and political causes.

In 1938, Lord MacLeod was inspired to rebuild the community on the Isle of Iona, a community that was first founded by Saint Columba in the sixth century, which had been a great monastic center of learning. Many Celtic monks, those "wandering saints," were sent forth from Iona during the early Middle Ages to teach and preach. They got as far as Kiev! Lord MacLeod sought to rekindle the spirit of the ancient Iona monastic center. He gathered a group of working-class men and then began the rebuilding of the ruined abbey. Today, the Iona Community has dispersed; there are associates of the community throughout the world. Many pilgrims make their way to Iona year after year, desiring to come together in a sacred place that was and is dedicated to a gospel of peace.

Lord MacLeod also wrote poetry and essays. His distinctive awareness of Christ's presence in and through all that is created is a hallmark of his written work.

John Philip Newell and John O'Donohue

Currently, there are a variety of authors whose work reflects the spirit of this tradition. John Philip Newell, Canadian by birth and living in Scotland, and his wife, Ali, were co-wardens of the Iona Community. Newell's historical work traces the continuity of Celtic spirituality from the time of Pelagius, to John Scotus Eriugena, to the Hebridean people, to George MacLeod, George MacDonald, and other Scots writers. Newell has also given us several beautiful books of prayers that are thoroughly steeped in the insights and cadences of this tradition. His work exemplifies the ancient wisdom that our prayer shapes our faith, and that faith shaped by prayer deepens us in compassion and delight in God's good gifts.

The late John O'Donohue, an Irish writer, poet, and philosopher, wrote about the Celtic practice of having a soul friend (see page 103). O'Donohue was an Irish speaker who lived in the west of Ireland, in an area where English was spoken far less than the native tongue. His writing reflects the knowing that comes from speaking the language of the land. Playful and profound, lighthearted but kindly attentive to sorrow and loss, O'Donohue's books remind us that life itself is blessing, and that being alive is a miracle we never fully comprehend.

Creation

Celtic Christian spirituality came to me through a woman mentor and friend. Her gift of those prayer anthologies led me into these vast, rich, and varied expressions of Christian faith, both historical and contemporary. Immediately upon praying those prayers, I discovered that they voiced an awareness of the creation that I had yearned for without realizing how strong the yearning was. The whole created order is not only named and included in these prayers. The created order, from smallest particle to furthest star, is recognized as an active agent of God's own goodness and mercy. God's blessing, majesty, and creativity are revealed through earth, sea, sky, wind, plants, and creatures. This spirituality directly refutes any splitting of matter and spirit. Celtic spirituality is notable for its supreme confidence that this cosmos is in God, and that if it were not in God, it simply could not, would not, exist. In this respect, the way of Celtic Christian spirituality follows in the way of the Hebrew Scriptures and in some ways sounds very Jewish. Further, this is a spirituality that confidently affirms that matter is of God—every speck of it, every quark, every not-yet-named particle.

Prayer and Daily Life

At the time that these prayers entered my life, I was raising two sons, keeping house for my family of four, and tending a small congregation in a rural town in central Texas. As a newly ordained priest in the Episcopal Church, I also performed a round of the ordinary rhythms of domestic chores—grocery shopping, meal preparation, house cleaning, laundry, tending the dogs. At a point when it would have been so easy to denigrate those activities in favor of the public priestly role I was beginning to live, the prayers emphatically led me to remember God's presence *right there*—right there amid the dishes and the dirty shirts, the dust bunnies and the dog bowls. Following the prayer and practice of the Christian East, with which the Celtic churches had early ties, this spirituality affirms that "there is no place where God is not."[5] The daily rounds of home and family, work and leisure are the very places where God's presence is known and received. The prayers challenged me to shift my gaze, to stop seeking God's presence in the spectacular or the unusual. Instead, this way of praying allowed that hankering for more stimulation to ease up. I found a gentle redirecting of my attention to the wonder found close at hand. The more I read and the more I studied, the more I came to see life as whole, every moment woven into an infinitely beautiful design. In a culture in which we experience disconnections—work from home, personal from communal, economic from spiritual—this expression of Christian spirituality reflects deep assurance that everything is connected by Christ and with Christ and in Christ.

A deep healing comes through the restoration of this compelling vision, a vision that Jesus proclaimed and lived.

The Gift of the Body

By extension, and somewhat surprisingly, Celtic Christian spirituality perceives the body to be both a gift and a sign of God's goodness, and worthy of God's attention and protection. As you will discover in reading "The Breastplate of Laidcenn" (page 55), no part of the body is considered shameful. No aspect of our physical life is beyond the reach of grace and mercy. The physical, embodied life we live is a good life, a life offered as blessing by God. It is also a life that is, by its very nature, mortal. This Celtic Christian way reminds us repeatedly that our earthly lives are embodied lives, and that those very bodies are God's creation and God's dwelling place. At the same time, there is clarity about our numbered days, and about the fact that we all eventually die. We receive the gift of remembering that we are creatures. We are recalled to the awareness that we are God's handiwork. We are directed toward the wisdom of the psalmist: "So teach us to count our days that we may gain a wise heart" (Psalm 90:12).

"The Great Cloud of Witnesses"

This transitory life on Earth is in continuity with our life in the Risen Lord once we die. While on the one hand recognizing the unique and startling separation that death presents, this tradition proclaims on the other hand that we are always in the company of the "great cloud of witnesses" (Hebrews 12:1), even going so far as to suggest that those who now live in eternity are with us whether we are in our kitchens, our workplaces, our backyards, or our gardens. Celtic Christian spirituality has little or no use for the spiritual path of "the alone to the alone." This way of spiritual life and practice perceives that even when we may find ourselves in a solitary context, we are in the company of Christ and the saints, and that company is present to guide, inspire, protect, and celebrate.

Prayer Is Life and Life Is Prayer

In ways similar to the traditions from the desert mothers and fathers from the third to sixth centuries in Egypt and the Holy Land, Celtic Christian spirituality sees prayer and theology as intertwined and inseparable. Prayer and theology are two faces of a single reality. How we pray shapes our faith and practice.[6] And our prayed belief forms our actions in the world. Being becomes doing, in this case doing in the name of Jesus. As a consequence, this spirituality remembers that perception (how we see) has everything to do with forming our *way* of seeing. What we see will determine what we are willing to engage, serve, and attend. Prayer, in other words, is a humbling encounter with God's own Spirit within us, showing us our blindness and deafness to others. Prayer is one means by which we allow ourselves to be vulnerable enough to seek the healing of old wounds and repent for actions that have hurt us and others. Prayer is also an ever-joyful openness to God's presence in and through every person and every aspect of our lives.

Theological Anthropology

All of this, in its own way, raises the question of "theological anthropology." What is it to be a human being, to be in human community, in relationship to God? Various voices from this tradition strongly contend that human beings truly are made in the image and likeness of God, as scripture states (Genesis 1:26). Most seekers who begin to explore a spiritual path are asking, in some way or another, Who am I, and why am I here? The Celtic Christian tradition is very clear: the human family is made in the image and likeness of God. Because God is infinitely good and creative, we as God's creation bear those capacities. Whether or not we choose to live out those capacities, to offer them for the common good, is a matter of being humble enough to seek counsel and direction for the trajectory of our lives.

Soul Friends

Each of us needs the counsel and friendship of someone who knows us well, someone who can encourage us to notice behaviors that are destructive to ourselves and one another. Each of us needs a soul friend, an *anam cara* (Irish) or *periglour* (Welsh), who will guide us in growing in the likeness of God. As we grow in the likeness of God, our life, both as individuals and as communities, is marked more and more distinctly by faith, hope, and love. We grow in self-control. We exhibit the joy that is birthed only after deep sorrow. We know that with endurance we gain our souls. We trust that nothing is ever beyond the reach of God's mercy and healing.

Pilgrimage

This Christian way is a pilgrimage, a journey ever deeper into the virtues of faith, hope, and love. We make this pilgrimage as a company. We who travel together experience both the common journey and the singular, personal process as we practice living and praying. Our ultimate destination is the home we never leave, Jesus who walks with us and indwells us. The way becomes known to us in the daily walking of it. "Each day, each night, each light, each dark" (*Carmina Gadelica*, III, 77) we make our way together, that way being both shared and singular.

Blessing as a Way of Life

Celtic Christian spirituality is ultimately a way of blessing. "Blessing," in its Hebrew root meaning (*b-r-k*, as in *berakhah*), has to do with bending the knee. In *The Carmina Gadelica*, the collection of prayers from the Outer Hebrides compiled by Andrew Carmichael at the end of the nineteenth century, we find notes that men would "bend the knee" to the rising sun, and women would "bend the knee" to the new moon.[7] In each case, this was a sign of being humbled by the evidence of the presence and creative design of the great "God of life." Following in the way of Celtic Christian spirituality opens us to the wonder of life and to the humility to look beyond particular events and moments in the natural world to the God who is revealed in those events and moments. The Celtic Christian path both honors and celebrates the human capacity for learning and study while acknowledging that we are not the authors of all that has been made. This is the blessing of remembering that we are creatures, brought forth into an earthly home not of our making, and heading toward a reunion with the Holy One in whom we dwell and who dwells within us.

The Issue of Original Texts

All of the texts in this book are in English. I did not translate them. I do not speak, read, or write Welsh, Gaelic, Irish, Breton, or Cornish. This collection is a sampling of a much grander feast. I have been the recipient of work done by scholars who speak the native languages, and I am handing that good work on to you, the reader. Scholars such as Oliver Davies and Fiona Bowie, Thomas O'Loughlin, Noel Dermot O'Donoghue, A. M. Allchin, Esther de Waal, Patrick Thomas, and Saunders and Cynthia Davies have been my teachers, both in person and through their texts. I've had the privilege of teaching their texts at the Seminary of the Southwest in Austin, Texas, and in a variety of parish, diocesan, and conference settings for the past twenty years. My own work is derivative; since I do not have fluency in any of these native Celtic tongues, I am grateful for the careful work of translation that is being done.

This small collection is a place to begin, and within it there are treasures that will invite you to enter the astoundingly beautiful landscape of Celtic Christian spirituality. A way that remembers that we dwell in the Holy One who has already made us one, this Celtic manner of being and doing draws us into that vision from the Letter of Paul to the Colossians. We see anew the Christ who holds all things together (Colossians 1:17a), and the veil parts, showing us creation shimmering with the presence of the divine Light in which all exists, which sustains every bit of matter from moment to moment, and which transforms us, from the inside out, into human persons and human community, growing steadily into the image and likeness of God. The vision opens our souls to the practice of vulnerable, undefended humility and willingness to be made new. We recover the courage to be compassionate. We engender generosity in one another. We become acutely aware that our daily lives are lived in the presence of Jesus and the great cloud of witnesses. Faith becomes what it was always meant to be: living a way of love, walking a path of life, for the life of the world.

1 □ Creation

The Celtic Christian tradition distinctively regards the creation as intimately related to humankind. We all come from the same Source, and therefore have a shared origin in God, who speaks all that exists into being. This sense of the natural world being full of kith and kin does not, however, lead to a romanticized view. Far from it. Nature is given its due as *other*. Although humankind and the natural world are both the creative work of God, the natural world is full of mystery and power. In the selections that follow, you will discover a lively sense of a world thrumming with divine Presence, and a deeply respectful awe before the majestic works not of our making.

This is prayer rooted in an unshakable confidence that the world is of God, that the world is in Christ, and that the deep-down goodness of this world is the true reality. God is the world's origin and destination. So, far from being a tradition characterized by fuzzy romanticism or misty hopes, Celtic Christianity is grounded in the keen vision that perceives all matter as evidence of the creative activity of God.

Some scholars have said that the pre-Christian scripture of the Celts is the created world. It is certainly the case that in this tradition there is strong evidence of an awareness of the natural world, and a deep appreciation of the natural cycles: dark/light, winter/spring/summer/fall. The Celtic Christian tradition, ever mindful that we live our human lives within the vast habitat of the created order, reminds us that to forget that habitat is to forget the essence of our humanity.

Further, this vast habitat is a "book," a text spoken forth by God at every moment. The earth and all who dwell therein, the galaxies and stars, the universe beyond our comprehending—these are outward and visible signs of God's own breath and life, continually uttered into being by the Holy One whom we know in Jesus and through the Holy Spirit.

1 The eternal light is the uncreated light from which all that is comes forth. "The light shines in the darkness, and the darkness did not overcome it" (John 1:5). This is the light of God's own presence, illumining all that is.

2 This eternal, uncreated light is the essence of every speck of matter, every particle, every proton, every electron, each not-yet-named subatomic bit.

3 The Celtic Christians discerned that divine revelation is offered to humanity through two different books: the book of scripture and the book of the creation. In order to live in such a way that our lives mirror God's own life, we humans need to attend to both of these texts. Reading scripture without attention to the book of creation results in distortion. Reading creation without attention to scripture results in distortion. Only when the two are read together and allowed to speak in our hearts and souls, as well as our minds, do we begin to walk in a path of life.

4 When Eriugena speaks of "creatures," he means all that is animate. He also includes anything that has been created, that is not infinite in its nature. Anything that has a beginning and an end would be in the category of "creature."

5 The physical senses are God-given, and as such, they are the means by which we may perceive this Light at any given moment, in and through the created context of our lives.

Now the eternal light[1] manifests itself to the world[2] in two ways, through the Bible and creatures.[3] For the divine knowledge cannot be restored in us except by the letters of scripture and the sight of creatures.[4] Learn the words of scripture and understand their meaning in your soul; there you will discover the Word. Know the forms and beauty of sensible things by your physical senses,[5] and see there the Word of God. And in all these things Truth itself proclaims to you only he who made all things, and apart from whom there is nothing for you to contemplate since he is himself all things. He himself is the being of all things.

JOHN SCOTUS ERIUGENA,
HOMILY ON THE PROLOGUE TO THE GOSPEL OF JOHN

6   A theophany is a showing of divine presence. The uncreated light that holds all creation in being may awaken our awareness at any time or place. Any creature may teach us of God.

7   God indwells all that has been brought forth by divine love and intent. The creation exists because it is in God, in the risen Jesus, in the Holy Spirit. The creation would not *be* if it were not in God, because the eternal light and life are the essential foundation of all that is. God is immanent within the creation, but is in no way limited to the creation.

8   God transcends all that God brings forth at all times and in all places. God, being God, cannot be collapsed into the material world, or even into the world of spirit. God is beyond all of our thoughts, our metaphors, our speech. God is even beyond the word "God."

9   All is within God, who gives being because of God's own nature and essence. God cannot *not* give being. God also offers the lavish gift of well-being, continually inviting the whole created order to participate fully in life and Light. Eriugena is reflecting on the Prologue to the Gospel of John:

> In the beginning was the Word, and the Word was with God, and the Word was God. He was in the beginning with God. All things came into being through him, and without him not one thing came into being. What has come into being in him was life, and the life was the light of all people. The light shines in the darkness and the darkness did not overcome it. (John 1:1–5)

Every visible and invisible creature can be called a
theophany.[6]

> JOHN SCOTUS ERIUGENA, *PERIPHYSEON: ON THE DIVISION OF NATURE*

We should not therefore understand God and creation as
two different things, but as one and the same.[7] For creation
subsists in God, and God is created in creation in a
remarkable and ineffable way, manifesting Himself, and
though invisible, making Himself visible, and though
incomprehensible, making Himself comprehensible, and
though hidden, revealing Himself, and though unknown,
making Himself known.[8]

> JOHN SCOTUS ERIUGENA, *PERIPHYSEON: ON THE DIVISION OF NATURE*

Likewise the beginning is the very being which is God,
who grants being and gives well-being as a gift, and is truly
the Beginning and the End.[9]

> JOHN SCOTUS ERIUGENA, *PERIPHYSEON: ON THE DIVISION OF NATURE*

10 The Celtic Christian tradition perceives that the creation itself offers praise to God. The sea, the sky, the trees, the animals, the stars—all these are seen to be continually speaking the praise of God, but without human speech. It is the vocation of the whole of creation to praise God, not only in song and poetry, but also in living creatively within the divine design and pattern. We can never exhaust our praise, nor can we ever capture the fullness of God's presence and gift in our prayer.

11 The world itself is a stunning miracle. The diversity of creatures, plants, and habitats on this earth, and the stunning array of the heavens, all lead us to be caught up in wonder.

12 This God, seen in and through Jesus, is the God who makes us whole. The root meaning of the word "save" in New Testament Greek is "making whole" or "healing." God saves us by giving us the gift of life, and by deepening our awareness of the small but essential part that each of us has in the intricate patterns of creation.

Almighty Creator
Almighty Creator, it is you who have made
the land and the sea....

The world cannot comprehend in song bright and
    melodious,
even though the grass and trees should sing,
all your wonders, O true Lord![10]

The Father created the world by a miracle;
it is difficult to express its measure.
Letters cannot contain it, letters cannot comprehend it.[11]

Jesus created for the hosts of Christendom,
with miracles when he came,
resurrection through his nature.

He who made the wonder of the world,
will save us, has saved us.[12]
It is not too great a toil to praise the Trinity.

Clear and high in the perfect assembly,
let us praise above the nine grades of angels
The sublime and blessed Trinity.

(continued on page 27)

13 When we praise God, both in song and in poetry, and by our actions, we are joined by the spiritual beings: angels, archangels, and the whole company of heaven. For our empirical minds, this may be difficult to embrace. The Celtic Christian tradition is mindful of the limits of our intelligence and our perception, and invites us to allow for the possibility of beneficent spiritual presences who guide and accompany us.

14 "Breastplate prayers" or "loricas" invoke God's presence as a shield or a breastplate of armor, following the language of the Letter of Paul to the Ephesians: "Put on the whole armor of God" (Ephesians 6:11, RSV).

15 This version of "The Deer's Cry," often attributed to Saint Patrick, calls on the natural world itself as an agent of the risen life of Jesus. Heaven, the sun, the moon, fire, lightning, wind, ocean, earth, rock— all are evidence of God's own presence in and through God's creation. A very early hymn from the first days of the Christian church, found in the Letter of Paul to the Colossians, also offers this insight: "All things have been created through him [Christ] and for him. He himself is before all things, and in him all things hold together" (Colossians 1:16b–17).

Purely, humbly, in skillful verse,
I should love to give praise to the Trinity,
according to the greatness of his power.
God has required of the host in this world
who are his, that they should at all times,
all together, fear the Trinity.

The one who has power, wisdom and dominion
Above heaven, below heaven, completely,
It is not too great toil to praise the Son of Mary.[13]

NINTH CENTURY, OLD WELSH

Breastplate of Saint Patrick
For my shield this day I call:[14]
    Heaven's might,
    Sun's brightness,
    Moon's whiteness,
    Fire's glory,
    Lightning's swiftness,
    Wind's wildness,
    Ocean's depth,
    Earth's solidity,
    Rock's immobility.[15]

SEVENTH CENTURY, IRISH

16 An *englyn* is a form of poetry in Welsh that follows particular rules of rhyme and meter. The writer imagines that the song of the thrush is a poem, inspired by God.

17 The thrush's wings, and the setting in this grove, recall the beauty of gathering for communion. The bird's vesture of feathers recalls the beauty of the attire worn by the Christian priest when celebrating Mass (Holy Communion). The "altar" within this natural setting calls to mind the altar within a church. Throughout Celtic Christian poems and writings, the first cathedral of worship is found in nature. Churches and cathedrals are places of shelter and gathered community, set within the great cathedral of creation. The sacredness of the entire creation, indwelt by God's own presence, is focused and recalled by those buildings.

18 The "gospel without haste" is the word of God offered through this book of creation, offered in the rhythms and seasons—day/night, light/dark, winter/spring/summer/fall.

19 The leaf recalls the wafer, the bread of Holy Communion. The poet is led to see that the pattern of communion is embedded in the pattern of creation. The pattern of taking, blessing, breaking, and distributing is God's own life visible in and through the ritual at the altar and in the life of the natural world.

The Mass of the Grove

I was in a pleasant place today
Beneath mantles of fine, green hazel,
Listening at break of day
To the skillful cock thrush
Singing a splendid englyn[16]
Of fluent signs and lessons.
He is a stranger here, of wise nature,
Love's brown go-between from afar,
From fair Carmarthenshire he came
At my golden girl's command.
Full of words, without password,
He makes his way to Nentyrch valley;
It was Morfudd who sent him,
Foster son of May, skilled in the arts of song,
Swathed in the vestments
Of flowers of the sweet boughs of May,
His chasuble was of the wings,
Green mantles of the wind.
By the great God, there was here
Only gold for the altar's canopy.[17]
In bright language I heard
A long and faultless chanting,
An unfaltering reading to the people
Of the gospel without haste,[18]
And on the hill for us there
Was raised a well-formed leaf as wafer,[19]

(continued on page 31)

20 The Sanctus bell is rung at the moment in the Mass when these words are chanted: "Holy, holy, holy, Lord God of Hosts, heaven and earth are full of your glory" (Isaiah 6:3). In the context of this poem, that chant is offered by creation—by the nightingale in this particular instance. All the world—the entire cosmos—sings, "Holy, holy, holy."

21 The poet hears the blackbird's song as praise, as a poem raised in offering to God. All the creatures offer praise in their own way.

22 This hermit-poet is reading and writing while listening to the bird. In all probability, the text he reads is some portion of the Bible. The book would have been made by hand. Reading, writing, reflecting, and praying are all within the context of the greenwood. The poet's habitat directly forms and informs his prayer and his engagement with scripture.

23 The Celtic Christian tradition speaks of "thin spaces"—geographical contexts in which the interdependent nature of heaven and earth is keenly sensed. Upon encountering a thin space, we are greeted by the ever-present community of angels, archangels, and all the company of heaven. The material world is shot through with intimations of divine presence. In some landscapes, the veil between the earthly sphere and the heavenly sphere is very thin.

And the slender, eloquent nightingale
From the corner of a nearby grove,
Poetess of the valley, rings out to the many
The Sanctus bell in her clear whistle,[20]
Raising the sacrifice on high to the sky above the bush,
With adoration to God the Father,
And with a chalice of ecstasy and love.
This psalmody pleases me:
Bred it was by a gentle grove of birch trees.

DAFYDD AP GWILYM, FOURTEENTH CENTURY, WALES

The Scribe in the Woods

A hedge of trees surrounds me, a blackbird's lay sings to me,
    praise I shall not conceal,[21]
Above my lined book the trilling of the birds sings to me.
A clear-voiced cuckoo sings to me in a grey cloak from the
    tops of the bushes.
May the Lord save me from Judgement; well do I write
    under the greenwood.[22]

NINTH CENTURY, OLD IRISH

The Lord of Creation

Let us adore the Lord,
Maker of marvelous works,
Bright heaven with its angels,
And on earth the white-waved sea.[23]

NINTH CENTURY, OLD IRISH

24 The mistle thrush is an outward and visible sign, a sacramental sign—an embodied expression—of God's own creative love, which sustains everything that exists from moment to moment. The poet begins his prayer-poem with attentive focus on this small bird, recognizing in its beauty and song the handiwork of God.

25 Not only is the mistle thrush a sacramental sign, but the bird is also an evangelist who preaches the good news of God's love for all that God has brought forth into being, and God's infinite care for every aspect of the material world. The bird's song, a gospel of good news in and of itself, recalls Jesus, who spoke of God's care for the "birds of the air" (Matthew 10:26).

26 A bird offers a sermon! Preaching does not need to be in words. In fact, the embodiment of faith, hope, and love in daily living is the best sermon that one may hear or offer. The poet reminds us that God's own life is incarnate, embodied in and through the instruments of a diverse and wondrous creation.

The Mistle Thrush
Lowly bird, beautifully taught,
You enrich and astound us,
We wonder long at your song,
Your artistry and your voice.
In you I see, I believe,
The clear and excellent work of God.[24]
Blessed and glorious is he,
Who shows his virtue in the lowest kind.
How many bright wonders (clear note of loveliness)
Does the world contain? How many parts, how many
    mirrors of his finest work
Offer themselves a hundred times to our gaze?
For the book of his art is a speaking light
Of lines abundantly full,
And every day one chapter after another
Comes among us to teach us of him.[25]
The smallest part of his most lovely hand
Finely taught our teacher,
A winged and lively bird,
Who gave an impromptu sermon,[26]
Who taught us much
Of the Lord who is Master,
Of right measure, his power and wealth,
And wisdom, great and true.
Let us come to receive his learning,
Unmerited, from this learned bird:

(*continued on page 35*)

27 Having been led to this sense of wonder through the agency of the
mistle thrush, the poet realizes that pondering the whole of creation
will lead us to astonishment. How can it be that so much loveliness
exists? How is it that there is something instead of nothing?

28 The course of this prayer then leads the poet to that awareness that
not only is his capacity to praise God for all aspects of creation inade-
quate, but the poet will also never be able to fully name, describe, or
discover the infinite goodness and beauty of God. His prayer begins
with prayerful attention to the mistle thrush and to God's immanent
presence in and through the bird. The reflection leads the poet to that
moment of profound silence and adoration when praise has been
offered in body, mind, and spirit, and we know anew that God is
always more than what we can ask or imagine.

Let the Lord be praised (by his own right),
Holy and pure, and no idol.
If our Lord is great, and great his praise
From just his one small part of earth,
Then what of the image of his greatness
Which comes from the whole of his fine work?[27]
And through the image of the ascending steps
Of his gracious work, which he has made,
(Below and above the firmament,
Marvellously beyond number),
What of the greatness and pure loveliness
Of God himself?[28]

THOMAS JONES, EIGHTEENTH-CENTURY
METHODIST MINISTER, WALES

29 This prayer comes from *The Carmina Gadelica*, a collection of prayers and chants from the oral tradition of the Outer Hebrides, islands off the northwest coast of Scotland, compiled by Alexander Carmichael in the late nineteenth century. Carmichael wrote down the prayers that had been handed down from father to son, mother to daughter, in oral tradition, then compiled and translated them. The robust faith of the Celtic people shines through in this collection. This particular prayer comes from a woman from the Isle of Harris who suffered from leprosy. She gathered plants and shellfish, boiled them together, and bathed herself with the broth. Over time, her skin became like new.

30 This stanza demonstrates that the woman who composed the prayer knew the story from the Gospel of Matthew in which Jesus curses a fig tree, which then withers (Matthew 21:18–22, also in Mark 11:12–14). She has known withering in her own flesh and is hopeful that the withering of her leprous condition may be transformed.

31 She proclaims the goodness of the plants, the animals, the sea, the sky, all of which are "in Christ." The whole creation is sustained by God at every single instant, and because of that immediate presence in and through the elements of matter, we may discover the means of healing in the natural world that surrounds us.

Jesus Who Ought to Be Praised

It were as easy for Jesu[29]
To renew the withered tree
As to wither the new
Were it His will so to do.
    Jesu! Jesu! Jesu!
    Jesu! meet it were to praise Him.[30]

There is no plant in the ground
But is full of His virtue,
There is no form in the strand
But is full of His blessing.
    Jesu! Jesu! Jesu!
    Jesu! meet it were to praise Him.

There is no life in the sea,
There is no creature in the river,
There is naught in the firmament,
But proclaims His goodness.
    Jesu! Jesu! Jesu!
    Jesu! meet it were to praise Him.

There is no bird on the wing,
There is no star in the sky,
There is nothing beneath the sun,
But proclaims His goodness.
    Jesu! Jesu! Jesu!
    Jesu! meet it were to praise Him.[31]

THE CARMINA GADELICA, I, 39–41

32 | This prayer from *The Carmina Gadelica* offers a sacramental vision of the sun itself. From the earliest days of the Christian faith, the sun was linked with the Son of God, Jesus who is the Christ, the Messiah, the Anointed One. Upon seeing the dawn, people of the Outer Hebrides would offer this prayer, reminding themselves, as they beheld the sun's appearance, that God was beholding them gently and generously. As the "eye of God" made its daily dawning, that natural rhythm proved to be an occasion for remembering God's ordering of those rhythms.

33 | Without the light of the sun, crops would not grow, fruit would not set, animals would not breed. The light of the sun is essential to the life of the earth. On a primal level, this prayer reminds us of the rhythms of light and dark that we take for granted in our twenty-first-century society.

The Eye of the Great God
The eye of the great God,[32]
The eye of the God of glory,
The eye of the King of hosts,
The eye of the King of the living,
    Pouring upon us
    At each time and season,
    Pouring upon us
    Gently and generously.

        Glory to thee,
            Thou glorious sun,
        Glory to thee, thou sun,
            Face of the God of life.[33]

                                    THE CARMINA GADELICA, III, 307

34 From the Irish hermit tradition, this short poem offers us a window into a life in which prayer, nature, and the work of human hands are woven together. St. Gobban was a master architect of the seventh century in Ireland who is reputed to have built many oratories and hermitages. Gobban's work was in partnership with the risen Jesus; the two of them were co-laborers in the thatching of the roof.

35 In a time of tribal war and unpredictable moments of violence, the hermit senses that this hut is set apart as a place of peace and stability. The everlasting, uncreated light is present in this small home where prayer, nature, and human labor weave a tapestry of life offered to God.

The Ivy Crest
In Tuaim Inbhir here I find
No great house such as mortals build,
A hermitage that fits my mind
With sun and moon and starlight filled.

'Twas Gobban shaped it cunningly
—This is a tale that lacks not proof—
And my heart's darling in the sky,
Christ, was the thatcher of its roof.[34]

Over my house rain never falls,
There comes no terror of the spear;
It is a garden without walls
And everlasting light shines here.[35]

NINTH CENTURY, OLD IRISH

36 Pelagius, a Christian monk, wrote in the late fourth and early fifth centuries. A native Briton, he emphasized that we come forth from God and carry within us the life of the Holy One who brings us into being, knitting us together in our mothers' wombs (Psalm 139:13). His writings recall the Prologue to the Gospel of John: "All things came into being through him [Christ], and without him not one thing came into being" (John 1:3). Because all things come into being through the life of the risen Jesus, all things are in him, and therefore potentially revelatory of God's power and presence.

37 Pelagius invites us to behold the natural world from a spiritual perspective, marveling at the abundant diversity that surrounds us, and reverently beholding a world that we did not create. His vision is of a world that is held together by God's power and creative goodness at every single moment. It is a vision that causes us to halt our consuming ways. We are led to behold the natural world, and the habitats in which we live, with a loving gaze that mirrors God's own way of beholding what God has brought forth.

God is present in all things, great and small. God's power is manifest in all events, great and small.[36]

PELAGIUS, *LETTER TO DEMETRIAS*

Look at the animals roaming the forest: God's spirit dwells within them. Look at the birds flying across the sky: God's spirit dwells within them. Look at the tiny insects crawling in the grass: God's spirit dwells within them. Look at the fish in the river and sea: God's spirit dwells within them. There is no creature on earth in whom God is absent. Travel across the ocean to the most distant land, and you will find God's spirit in the creatures there. Climb up the highest mountain, and you will find God's spirit among the creatures who live at the summit. When God pronounced that his creation was good, it was not only that his hand had fashioned every creature; it was that his breath had brought every creature to life. Look too at the great trees of the forest; look at the wild flowers and the grass in the fields; look even at your crops. God's spirit is present within all plants as well. The presence of God's spirit in all living beings is what makes them beautiful; and if we look with God's eyes, nothing on the earth is ugly.[37]

PELAGIUS, *LETTER TO AN ELDERLY FRIEND*

38 Pelagius tells us to stretch our imaginations, our souls, and our hearts when we hear the Great Commandment: "You shall love the Lord your God with all your heart, and with all your soul, and with all your strength, and with all your mind; and your neighbor as yourself" (Deuteronomy 6:5, Leviticus 19:18, Luke 10:27). Our sense of the neighbor must include all the flora and fauna in the habitat in which we live. Were we to follow this instruction, our actions would reflect our mindfulness of consequences for our plant and animal neighbors. We would be faithfully attending to the ecosystems in which we live, and to all who inhabit them.

39 The Celtic Christian tradition is wary of identifying the creation with God. That said, Pelagius and other Celtic teachers were clear that the creation exists because God creates it, loves it, and holds it in being. Were that not the case, the creation would cease to be. Every place is holy ground, for every place is in the Holy One. Every space and time is an occasion for encountering God's love. If I love my dog, I care for my dog with kindness and attention. That kindness and attention is a way of participating in the fullness of God's love.

When Jesus commands us to love our neighbours, he does
not only mean our human neighbours; he means all the
animals and birds, insects and plants, amongst whom we
live. Just as we should not be cruel to other human beings,
so we should not be cruel to any other species of creature.
Just as we should love and cherish other human beings, so
we should love and cherish all God's creation.[38]

PELAGIUS, *A LETTER TO AN ELDERLY FRIEND*

Yet we should remember that all love comes from God; so
when our love is directed towards an animal or even a tree,
we are participating in the fullness of God's love.[39]

PELAGIUS, *A LETTER TO AN ELDERLY FRIEND*

40 The author of this poem, George F. MacLeod, was a Scots Presbyterian minister. Having fought in the trenches in World War I, he was headed home on a troop train with other wounded soldiers when he had a profound experience of Christ's presence. This led him to found the Iona Community on the Isle of Iona in the Hebrides. He was emphatic in his awareness that all matter is God's own handiwork: matter matters.

41 We come into God's house, a church or a sanctuary, mindful that God's creation is also God's house. Therefore, sky, sea, land, sun and planets, the earth, the wind—every aspect of creation—is a reminder of God's own immediate presence with us and surrounding us in all places and at all times.

42 We are called to behold the bounty around us, and to care for that natural world as God's own dwelling place. Animal husbandry, agriculture, gardening, forestry—all are ways of allowing us to tend and care for the natural world, which is not only a gift but also a book of divine revelation from which we may see God's own embodied Word in our midst.

43 Ireland, Scotland, Wales, Cornwall, Brittany, the Isle of Man, and Galicia are all lands whose people have turned to the sea for food, livelihood, recreation, and inspiration. Throughout the Celtic Christian writings, we hear a keen awareness of the rhythms of the sea and the currents of the ocean. These writers see in those rhythms and currents a kind of wisdom for life. We experience tidal rhythms in our own lives, rhythms not of our own making. Sometimes a strong current in politics or economics directly affects us. These tides and currents are part of the social and cultural habitat of our lives.

Eternal Seeping through the Physical (excerpt)
We come into Thy house, our home[40]
once more to give thanks:
for earth and sea and sky in harmony of colour,
the air of the eternal seeping through the physical,
the everlasting glory dipping into time.
We praise Thee.[41]

For nature resplendent:
growing beasts, mergent crops, singing birds,
and all the gayness of the green.
We bless Thee.[42]

For swift running tides, resistant waves, Thy spirit on the
      waters,[43]
the spirit of the inerrant will,
Striving with the currents that are also Thine.
We bless Thee.
O Lord: how marvelous are Thy works.
In majesty hast Thou created them.

GEORGE F. MACLEOD

2 ☐ Prayer

The Celtic Christian tradition, both historical and contemporary, leads us to see that every aspect of life may be brought to speech in prayer. This is a vision of life as ongoing prayer, and of prayer as all of life. It is all-encompassing and startling in its attention to the body, to the totality of the created world, to strangers and enemies. Underlying this vision is a profoundly ordinary contemplative way of seeing and being. In humble, daily ways, the book of creation comes under the attentive gaze of the human community. Guided by the insights and wisdom of scripture, that gazing leads to exuberant praise in poetry and song. The point of departure might be a bird singing its morning song or the rhythm of the waves in the Irish Sea. Kindly attention to these singular encounters in creation then opens us up to those deeper questions: Why is there anything at all? How is it that we are surrounded by life in its diverse forms on every side? How can it be that acts of kindness still persist amid violence?

This Celtic way of prayer, marked by distinctive cultural expressions (Hebridean, Welsh, Irish), leads us to the commonality of our human experience. We are reminded to pray through the ritual actions of our day. When we read of a woman blessing the kindling of the fire, that might lead us to offer a morning prayer as we prepare coffee. When we read of the blessing of the herd, that might lead us to pray more deeply for the creatures in our household and throughout the world.

Most of the prayers from this tradition are poems or songs. The lyric quality continues to the present day. Modern poets from Scotland, Ireland, Wales, Brittany, and Cornwall are crafting praise poems, poems that speak of loss and trials, poems that awaken our hearts and stir our souls.

1 The Celtic Christian tradition is rich with feminine metaphors for God. In this saying from the Hebrides, God's maternal love is proclaimed. Maternal love is primarily (though not limited to) love for the offspring of the mother's body. This tradition perceives humanity, and all that is, to be the issue of divine Love.

2 This traditional prayer from Ireland is also sung as a hymn by many Christian denominations. The prayer begins with an ancient cosmology, which perceived that there are seven heavens, the seventh being the place of God's deepest being, a place of ultimate joy and deep contentment. The "high king" in ancient Ireland was the king who ruled over all of the smaller kingdoms. In Irish song and prayer, Jesus is often referred to as the "high king," because his rule takes precedence over all other authorities.

3 The prayer voices that deepest of desires—that all of our being— body, mind, and spirit—be indwelt by God's own presence. Further, the prayer acknowledges that in both our waking hours and our sleeping hours God is with us. This is an essential dimension of the Christian gospel—that in Jesus God tells us that God is with us at all times and in all places. In other words, "There is no place where God is not."

4 This verse echoes the insights found in the Gospel of John (see John 14–17), the mystical awareness of mutual indwelling: that God dwells in us, and we dwell in God. At the same time, God is never reduced to the material world, for God is the source from which all things, visible and invisible, proceed.

5 The mutual indwelling is represented both in the language of parent and child and in the language of betrothal. God's love for us, and our love for God, may be spoken of with a rich variety of metaphors of the human experience of love.

6 When we allow ourselves to be increasingly attentive to the divine presence within us and around us, a steady formation takes hold, which allows us to entrust ourselves to God, no matter the circumstances in which we live.

Mother's Heart
There is a mother's heart in the heart of God.[1]

HEBRIDEAN SAYING

Be Thou My Vision
Be thou my vision, beloved Lord: none other is
Aught but the King of the seven heavens.[2]

Be thou my meditation by day and night;
May it be thou that I behold forever in my sleep.[3]

Be thou my speech; be thou my understanding;
Be thou for me: may I be for thee.[4]

Be thou my father: may I be thy son;
Mayst thou be mine, may I be thine.[5]

Be thou alone my special love;
Let there be none other save the High-King of heaven.

Thy love in my soul and in my heart—
Grant this to me, O King of the seven heavens.[6]

Beloved Christ, whate'er befall me,
O Ruler of all, be thou my vision.

TENTH OR ELEVENTH CENTURY, IRISH

7 A traditional encircling prayer, this prayer is offered while the petitioner slowly turns "sunwise," from east to west to east again. While that slow pivot is made, the petitioner often extends the right hand, or both hands, as a sign of offering. The practice of pivoting "sunwise" is an intentional recognition that we exist in a created order not of our making. It is a physical reminder of God's established rhythms and seasons.

8 This encircling prayer is a strong reminder of God's intimate, constant presence, whether we are awake or asleep, at work or at leisure.

An Encircling Prayer

My Christ! My Christ! My shield, my encircler,
Each day, each night, each light, each dark:
 My Christ! My Christ! My shield, my encircler,
 Each day, each night, each light, each dark.[7]

Be near me, uphold me, my treasure, my triumph,
In my lying, in my standing, in my watching, in my
 sleeping.[8]

Jesus, Son of Mary! My helper, my encircler,
Jesus, Son of David! My strength everlasting:
 Jesus, Son of Mary! My helper, my encircler,
 Jesus, Son of David! My strength everlasting.

THE CARMINA GADELICA, III, 77

9   Another example of a breastplate prayer (see also page 27), "The Breastplate of Laidcenn" begins with an explicit invocation of the Trinity. In traditional Celtic Christian prayers, the Trinity is often named, sometimes as "Unity in Trinity," sometimes as "the Three of my love," sometimes as "the sacred Three." The Celtic churches, following the practice of the early church, venerated the Trinity as revealing "God in three persons," traditionally named Father, Son, and Holy Spirit.

10   This breastplate is remarkable for its unabashed naming of the parts and organs of the body, seeking God's protection for every bit of anatomy. The full prayer includes all the inner organs. It reveals both an astounding awareness of our embodied selves and a trust in the God who has brought each of those organs into being.

The Breastplate of Laidcenn (excerpt)
Help me, Unity in Trinity,
Trinity in Unity, take pity....[9]

Deliver my skull, hair-covered head, and eyes,
Mouth, tongue, teeth and nostrils,
Neck, breast, side and limbs,
Joints, fat and two hands.

Be a helmet of safety to my head,
To my crown covered with hair,
To my forehead, eyes, and triform brain,
To snout, lip, face and temple,

To my chin, beard, eyebrows, ears,
Chaps, cheeks, septum, nostrils,
Pupils, irises, eyelids, and the like,
To gums, breath, jaws, gullet,

To my teeth, tongue, mouth, uvula, throat,
Larynx and epiglottis, cervix,
To the core of my head and gristle,
And to my neck may there be merciful protection.
Be then a most protective breastplate
For my limbs and innards,
So that you drive back from me the unseen
Nails of the shafts that foul fiends fashion.[10]

SEVENTH CENTURY, IRISH

11 This prayer and confession of faith comes from *The Carmina Gadelica*. It is the composition of a woman named Mary Gillies, who was illiterate, ill, and aged when Andrew Carmichael recorded her prayer. She sang it for him in Gaelic as a chant. This was her morning offering, her personal proclamation of faith in God, received from those in her family who had gone before. God is the One who brings forth life and love, and who dwells in eternity, infusing time with divine presence.

12 God is the creator of all that surrounds us, both what we can see and what we cannot see. Heaven and earth, the sky and the sea, and all that lives in those environments come forth from God.

13 Each human person is the handiwork of God, shaped by God's own intimate creative action. God is like a weaver, working with the warp threads of our souls—those strong vertical threads on a loom that are the deep structure of cloth upon which the design is woven. Many in the Hebrides made a living by raising sheep, shearing sheep, preparing wool, spinning, and weaving. The daily experience of those endeavors becomes active metaphors for prayer.

14 The formula "bless to me" is found throughout the prayers from the Hebrides. It is a way of stating a relationship with the God whose being is blessing. "Bless to me" names a reality that is ever present, and seeks an awareness of God's eternal presence and blessing in every aspect of life.

O God of All Gods

I believe, O God of all gods,
That Thou art the eternal Father of life:
I believe, O God of all gods,
That Thou art the eternal Father of love.[11]

I believe, O Lord and God of the peoples,
That Thou art the creator of the high heavens,
That Thou art the creator of the skies above,
That Thou art the creator of the oceans below.[12]

I believe, O Lord and God of the peoples,
That Thou art He who created my soul and set its warp.
Who created my body from dust and from ashes,
Who gave to my body breath and to my soul its
    possession.[13]

Father, bless to me my body,
Father, bless to me my soul,
Father, bless to me my life,
Father, bless to me my belief.[14]

THE CARMINA GADELICA, III, 45–47

15 This prayer from Ireland calls our attention to speech that is worthy of God. In our age of careless or hurtful speech, this prayer reminds us that all speech is in God's hearing. Our voices are intended for praise, poetry, and song. The prayer encourages us to be mindful of our speech, and to offer praise to the God who has made us.

16 Prayer in the Celtic Christian tradition is, at its core, an expression of joy. In part this is the result of the influence of the Gospel of John, in which Jesus speaks so clearly of his desire that his followers know joy (see John 3:29, 15:11, 16:20, 17:13). It is also a cultural predisposition, despite difficult and disastrous economic, social, and political circumstances. In these Celtic prayers we encounter a vision of God who joys in creating, joys in loving, joys in receiving us at the end of our earthly lives. It is a vision of humanity created for joy.

My Speech

My speech—may it praise you without flaw: May my heart
love you, King of heaven and earth.
My speech—may it praise you without flaw: Make it easy
for me, pure Lord, to do you all service and to adore
you.
My speech—may it praise you without flaw: Father of all
affection, hear my poems and my speech.[15]

TWELFTH CENTURY, IRISH

Fashioned for Joy

As the hand is made for holding and the eye for seeing,
thou hast fashioned me for joy. Share with me the vision
that shall find it everywhere: in the wild violet's beauty; in
the lark's melody; in the face of a steadfast man; in a child's
smile; in a mother's love; in the purity of Jesus.[16]

TRADITIONAL GAELIC, TRANSLATED BY ALISTAIR MACLEAN

17 This Irish prayer gives the petitioner a sense of the cross as a presence, an aspect of the presence of Jesus, risen and living, who is with us at all times and in all places, and who lived an earthly life. Our bodies are dear to him, and his cross is invoked as a protecting presence for body, mind, and spirit.

18 Just as Jesus is Emmanuel, God-with-us, so his cross is with us no matter which direction we travel. The cross of the risen Jesus is with us wherever we go, whatever we face, whomever we meet.

19 The cross is invoked as a protection against evil, rather like the breastplate prayers.

20 No part of the human body or person is outside the protecting presence of the cross.

Christ's Cross

Christ's cross over this face, and thus over my ear, Christ's
cross over this eye. Christ's cross over this nose.[17]

Christ's cross to accompany me before. Christ's cross to
accompany me behind me. Christ's cross to meet every
difficulty both on hollow and hill.

Christ's cross eastwards facing me. Christ's cross back
towards the sunset. In the north, in the south,
increasingly may Christ's cross straightway be.[18]

Christ's cross up to broad Heaven. Christ's cross down to
earth. Let no evil or hurt come to my body or my soul.[19]

Christ's cross over me as I sit. Christ's cross over me as I lie.
Christ's cross be all my strength until we reach the King
of Heaven.

From the top of my head to the nail of my foot, O Christ,
against every danger I trust in the protection of the
cross.[20]

Till the day of my death, going into this clay, I shall draw
without—Christ's cross over this face.

TENTH CENTURY, IRISH

21 This prayer, which comes from the Irish oral tradition, is often attrib-uted to St. Brigit, a fifth-century saint revered throughout Ireland, Scot-land, Wales, Cornwall, and Brittany. St. Brigit is known for her expansive hospitality and for her keen awareness of the needs of the poor. The prayer ends with a vision of a "great lake of beer," a vision of plenty, a vision of celebration and reunion.

22 The three Marys are mentioned in accounts of Jesus' death and res-urrection—Mary, the mother of Jesus; Mary Magdalene; and Mary, the mother of James. These women, who were with Jesus in both his dying and his risen life, would of course be present at a feast in heaven (see Mark 15:40–16:8; Matthew 27:55–56 and 28:1–10; Luke 8:1–3, 23:55–56, and 24:10–11; and John 19:25–27 and 20:1–18).

23 The feast of heaven would include one and all, because the Host, Jesus, calls all to the table to receive the bread and wine. This is a gath-ering of a vast company, celebrating ongoing life with one another and with Jesus.

24 This last verse resounds with the happy satisfaction of a woman who has gathered family to her table, fed them well, and been part of the celebration. A deep joy pervades the prayer, joy in Jesus' open hospital-ity, joy in the reunion with those who have died, joy in the sheer fact of being with one another.

The Banquet of Heaven
I would like to have the men of Heaven
In my own house:
With vats of good cheer
Laid out for them.[21]

I would like to have the three Marys,[22]
Their fame is so great.
I would like people
From every corner of Heaven.[23]

I would like them to be cheerful
In their drinking,
I would like to have Jesus too
Here amongst them.

I would like a great lake of beer
For the King of Kings,
I would like to be watching Heaven's family
Drinking it through all eternity.[24]

TENTH OR ELEVENTH CENTURY, TRADITIONAL IRISH

25 In this prayer poem from Welsh poet Waldo Williams, God is addressed directly in the second person "you." Each statement points us toward a different aspect of the mystery of God, who is closer to us than our breath, yet also infinitely beyond us, beyond the far reaches of the universe.

26 The Celtic Christian tradition has not been afraid to describe God's presence and work through metaphors founded in the elemental life of the earth: sun, fire, wind, water. The Welsh landscape, marked by hills, mountains, valleys, also has rivers that run ("flee") when heavy rain or snowmelt has swelled the waters.

27 Williams picks up the scriptural references to salt (see, for example, Matthew 5:13 and Luke 14:24). Salt draws out impurities and facilitates healing.

28 Again using a scriptural allusion (see 1 Corinthians 4:6 and 8:1), Williams notes our tendency toward pomposity, or "puffing up." God is the wind that pierces that illusion, and brings us to true humility.

29 The strong tradition of Christ being in the stranger is found throughout the Celtic lands. The traveler brings the disguised presence of the risen Jesus, and to refuse to answer the knock of the traveler is to refuse to welcome Him.

30 Each of us is also the home of the risen life of Jesus. Within us, in our deepest selves, this heavenly prince dwells, awaiting our awakening to the royal Presence at the core of our being, the Presence that gives us our true identity.

Knowing (*Adnabod*) (excerpt)
You are our breath. You are the flight
Of our longing to the depths of heaven.[25]
You are the water which flees from
The wilderness of our anxiety and fear.[26]
You are the salt which purifies.[27]
You are the piercing wind of our pomposity.[28]
You are the traveler who knocks.[29]
You are the prince who dwells within us.[30]

GORONWY (WALDO WILLIAMS), TWENTIETH-CENTURY POET, WALES,
TRANSLATED FROM THE WELSH BY NOEL DAVIES

31 The beginning of each day may gently stir us to growing awareness of God's image within us. God's own life, which holds together every particle of our being, is woven like golden thread into the fabric of that same being.

32 Our souls are fashioned to be like God, to be radiant with glory, to be alert for opportunities of self-giving love, to practice befriending all that God has brought into being.

33 Becoming more attentive to the "thread of glory" woven into all of life, we also see more clearly the behaviors that distort God's image within us. We awaken to God's own hope that we will receive the truth of our divine origin, and seek God's remedies for our weakness and distortion.

34 As we discern God's glory within ourselves, we also recall that every person, every animal, every bit of matter, springs forth from that same glory. The earth and the cosmos are revealed as God's own habitat, and therefore holy. The moral fiber within the fabric of our souls grows stronger, and we act in ways that honor God's presence in all places and at all times.

Opening Prayer
In the morning light, O God,
may I glimpse again your image deep within me
the threads of eternal glory
woven into the fabric of every man and woman.[31]
Again may I catch sight of the mystery of the human soul
fashioned in your likeness
deeper than knowing
more enduring than time.[32]
And in glimpsing these threads of light
amidst the weakness and distortions of my life
let me be recalled
to the strength and beauty deep in my soul.[33]
Let me be recalled
to the strength and beauty of your image in every living
soul.[34]

JOHN PHILIP NEWELL, TWENTY-FIRST CENTURY POET AND WRITER

3 □ Incarnation

The Word was made flesh and lived among us, and we have seen his
glory, the glory as of a father's only son.
—JOHN 1:14

Various scholars have remarked that for the pre-Christian Celts, the proclamation of the Word being made flesh was compatible with the awareness of matter being the work of divinity. From the Celtic perspective, matter was revelatory of divine creative action and was, in fact, potentially able to point us toward the Source from which the matter comes. It is hard to find dualistic theology in the Celtic Christian tradition. In contrast to some of the thinking and writing that was occurring in the Mediterranean Basin at the time of Pelagius (fourth and fifth centuries), the Celtic churches had no difficulty embracing the possibility that God became incarnate in Jesus.

We could say that Pelagius "comes on strong." He insists that because God becomes human in Jesus, we have been shown that all humans are to be treated with respect and dignity, and that material goods are to be distributed equitably (see chapter 7). Eriugena, writing three centuries later, is the beneficiary of later theological writing from the Christian east, which stressed the mystical life in Christ. Eriugena's thought and prayer may be challenging at first pass, especially for those who have not read patristic theology. Yet in these passages, we discover a man whose whole life has been captured by a vision of God's infinite goodness and mercy, revealed so kindly to us in Jesus.

1 This Christmas poem from a Welsh Franciscan friar draws us to that moment we know at Christmas Eve, the moment when we kneel before the manger, beholding this baby born in the poorest of circumstances, and open our hearts to receive the mystery of God born into our midst as Jesus. We also kneel before the truth that the birth points us toward: that each person is of God, each person is essentially holy, each person is brother or sister to the baby who lies in the straw.

2 Only the heart and soul can receive this Christmas revelation: God dwells fully, completely in a human baby. And this baby's life will tell us of what our lives might be if we awaken to the truth that we are always in God.

3 How can it be? In this tiny, vulnerable, poor newborn, weak and needy, hungering for milk and wearing a diaper, God shows us something of who God is. Words fail. Thoughts are insufficient. Adoration in silence and wonder draws us close to the heart of this babe.

4 The child is also Emmanuel, God-with-us. God is so intimately, immediately *with* us that God is willing to accept the limitation of being embodied. And God also desires to know human life from the inside out, from the moment of conception to the moment of death.

5 Jesus, who is the Christ, the Messiah, the Anointed One, bears none of the symbols of rank and power at his birth. He is found with the animals, the beasts that are often depicted as recognizing him as the Holy One in human form. The birth alerts us to God's presence among us in all places, and invites us to seek eyes to see and ears to hear, that we might pay attention to his presence among the sick, the lonely, the imprisoned, the orphaned, the grieving, the exiled.

Christmas Poem

Let us weigh wisely, let us wonder
   at
      Wonders accomplished,
Nothing more wondrous in this
   world ever
      Will men's lips tell of,[1]
God coming to us, He that created
   All of creation,
As God and as man, and God as a
   man,[2]
      Equally gifted.
Tremendous, tiny, powerful,
   feeble,
      Cheeks fair of colour,
Wealthy and needy, Father and
   Brother,
      Maker of Brothers,[3]
This, sure, is Jesus, whom we should welcome
   As Lord of rulers,
Lofty and lowly, Emmanuel,[4]
   Honey to think on.
An ox and an ass, the Lord of this world,
   A manger is His,
Bundle of hay instead of a cradle
   For our Lord of hosts.[5]

EXCERPT FROM A POEM BY MADAWG AP GWALLTER,
THIRTEENTH-CENTURY FRANCISCAN FRIAR, WALES

6 The Word becomes flesh, and the mystery of breath reveals to us the ongoing action of the God whose speaking is creative action. The breath of God's speaking reveals the Son and the Spirit, known to us through the life of Jesus. The breath of God's speaking is the essence of everything that exists, from the tiniest particle of subatomic matter to the farthest star. We come to this awareness in quiet meditation and reflection, allowing our minds to dwell in our hearts, opening to the movement of God's breathing in us and in the world.

Whoever speaks emits breath in the word that he utters; so too God the Father, at one and the same time, gives birth to his Son and, by the birth of the Son, produces the Spirit.[6]

JOHN SCOTUS ERIUGENA,
HOMILY ON THE PROLOGUE TO THE GOSPEL OF JOHN

7 The light of which Eriugena writes is the uncreated light, the light from which all matter pours forth and to which all matter returns. This vision draws us into a shimmering luminosity, a transfiguring splendor that is the essence of all that has been created and which is shown forth in the singular life of Jesus.

8 We abandon God every day, at all times and in all places. When we are blind to the light that sustains everything in being, we abandon the God who dwells within us, and we are blind to the Presence that upholds everything, seen and unseen, at every moment. Our lifelong pilgrimage is an invitation to gaze gently and steadily at present circumstance, watching for God's presence and guidance.

9 Following the instruction of some teachers in the early church, the Celtic tradition maintains that we are given two books of revelation: the small book of scripture and the vast book of creation. When we read one book without the other, we will inevitably miss the mark in our perception and our action. Only when we read both books, allowing both scripture and creation to be means through which God's breath and light are known, will we be able to discern, to decide, to act in ways that reflect awareness of God's mercies.

10 The early monastic communities of Ireland, Scotland, and Wales were centers of learning and knowledge. Books of gospels known as illuminated gospels (such as *The Book of Kells* and *The Book of Durrow*) were painstakingly created letter by letter. With color and design, the monks created illuminated manuscripts that effectively demonstrate both their love of scripture and their awareness that the Word of God speaks in and through the words of the Bible.

11 Following the wisdom of the Prologue to the Gospel of John ("All things came into being through him, and without him not one thing came into being" [John 1:3]), Eriugena points us toward the created order. When we allow ourselves to truly see the natural world with the "eyes of the heart," we awaken to the immediate and active presence of God, in and through matter.

He is light and therefore illumines himself, revealing himself to the world, manifesting himself to those who do not know him.[7]

The light of divine knowledge departed from the world when humankind abandoned God.[8] Now the eternal light manifests itself to the world in two ways, through the Bible and creatures.[9] For the divine knowledge cannot be restored in us except by the letters of scripture and the sight of creatures. Learn the words of scripture and understand their meaning in your soul; there you will discover the Word.[10] Know the forms and beauty of sensible things by your physical senses, and see there the Word of God.[11] And in all these things Truth itself proclaims to you only he who made all things, and apart from whom there is nothing for you to contemplate since he is himself all things. He himself is the being of all things.

JOHN SCOTUS ERIUGENA,
HOMILY ON THE PROLOGUE TO THE GOSPEL OF JOHN

12 The light of God brings us into being, sustains us, and receives us when we die. This light never fails to shine within us. Without this light, nothing would exist. This light dwells at the heart of each person, within the depths of all that has been created. This light is so vast that we cannot fully imagine it. And this light is the Love from which everything springs forth, and which holds everything in being.

13 This divine light is incipiently present in every person, even the most wicked and violent. Because it is divine light, it cannot be extinguished. Yet we have been given the freedom to deny this light, which is our origin and our end. We may choose to ignore it, denigrate it, or attempt to destroy it. Ultimately, however, "the Light shines in the darkness, and the darkness did not overcome it" (John 1:5).

14 Following teachers of the early church such as Dionysius the Areopagite and Maximus the Confessor, Eriugena restates an insight from the early church: that the human person is "microcosm and mediator." We are each a "little world," a microcosm. Our bodies (as contemporary science has demonstrated) are made up of elements from ancient stars, and within our bodies various organs exist as a planetary system of sorts. The body links us intimately to all creatures. The soul, the dimension of the person that is inextricably rooted and grounded in Light, is the dimension of ourselves that is incorporeal, not limited to the body.

15 The person is "mediator," a little universe that stands between the created world and the infinite love of divinity, of God. The human vocation, both as persons and as community, is to become increasingly aware of the linkage of earth and heaven, and to proclaim the mutual indwelling. Paying attention to signs of this mutual indwelling is our primary task, for it leads us to see, in the words of George MacLeod, that "matter matters" (John Philip Newell, *Listening to the Heartbeat of God* [New York: Paulist Press, 1997], p. 76).

The light shines in the darkness of the souls of the faithful, and the light increases, beginning with faith and ending with vision.[12] But the hearts of the unfaithful and the ignorant have not understood the light of the Word of God which shines in the flesh.[13]

JOHN SCOTUS ERIUGENA,
HOMILY ON THE PROLOGUE TO THE GOSPEL OF JOHN

It is only in the human person that this world is found, in whom all creatures are united. For we are composed of both body and soul.[14] Holding together the body of this world and the soul of the other world, we form a single universe. The body possesses the whole of corporeal nature and the soul the whole of incorporeal nature; united in a single whole, they constitute the entire universe of the self. That is why "man" is called "the whole," for all creatures are combined in him as in a vessel.[15]

JOHN SCOTUS ERIUGENA,
HOMILY ON THE PROLOGUE TO THE GOSPEL OF JOHN

16 This is the central mystery of the Christian faith: that in Jesus, God lived human life from the inside out, from birth to death. Yet more wonderful: we are shown our nature in its loveliest form, resplendent when deeply compassionate, transfigured when mindful of our home in God. Participation in God's life leads us to the truth in love, and to the dislodging of self-centered life.

17 Pelagius, blunt and concise as ever, reminds us that all our speculation will never comprehend the glory of God. Our best course is to follow Jesus, step by step, trusting that the path of love will lead us to where we are called to be.

The Word became flesh so that the flesh, that is, the human race, should ascend to him by believing in the Word through the flesh, so that through the natural, only-begotten Son many should be adopted as sons. Not for his own sake did the Word become flesh, but for our sake, who could not be changed into the sons of God except by the flesh of the Word. He came down alone but ascends with many. He who made of God a human being makes gods of men and women. *And dwelt among us*, that is, he took possession of our nature so that he might make us participators in his own nature.[16]

JOHN SCOTUS ERIUGENA,
HOMILY ON THE PROLOGUE TO THE GOSPEL OF JOHN

Do not let your mind be seduced by theological speculation; the human mind can never grasp the supreme glory of God. Simply follow Jesus wherever he leads.[17]

PELAGIUS, *LETTER TO DEMETRIAS*

4 □ Daily Life and Work

The Celtic tradition perceives God's presence in and through all of the minutiae of daily life. No moment in the daily round is so small that it cannot be an occasion of being encountered by God. No domestic chore is beyond adaptation to a means of prayer. These prayers offer us a vision of ordinary life made holy by an abounding, robust awareness of God's presence in every moment of every day, at every time in every season.

In addition, these prayers lead us to remember that the work we do, "the handling of our hands" (page 87), is done in partnership with the God who creates us and sets daily tasks before us. Our work is our means of making visible the bonds that unite us, and our means of honoring one another and God. The daily labor in which we engage, no matter how seemingly humdrum, is the very place in which we love both God and neighbor, in which we may offer ourselves for the common good.

Following the rhythms of awakening in the morning and going to sleep at night, the prayers also remind us of the rhythms and seasons of life. They recall for us the intricate and marvelous patterns in nature and in life cycles. We are directed to remember that we did not create those patterns and cycles; we are led to remember that it is God who has made us, and not we ourselves (Psalm 100:5).

1 Celtic Christian spirituality is distinctive in its embrace of the body. Our bodies are seen as gifts, and our bodies are known to be the means by which we act in the world, offering the love of God to those with whom we come in contact.

2 Like a Celtic knot from the designs of an illuminated gospel text, life and faith are woven together in an inseparable unity. The tie that links life to creed is a tie of love, a tie that links us both to God and to neighbor.

3 This prayer asks for a thorough soaking in God's grace, a soaking of such power that "every whit" of speech and thought, talk and intention, is informed by the divine love in which we live and move and have our being.

Body and Soul

Father, bless me in my body,
  Father, bless me in my soul;
Father, bless me this night
  In my body and in my soul.[1]

Father, bless me in my life,
  Father, bless me in my creed;
Father, bless me in my tie
  To my life and to my creed.[2]

Father, sanctify to me my speech,
  Father, sanctify to me my heart;
Father, sanctify to me every whit
  In my speech and in my heart.[3]

THE CARMINA GADELICA, III, 349

4 This Hebridean prayer begins with the affirmation that everything comes from God. Life itself is a gift, and prayer is a way of deepening our awareness of that essential truth. The gifted nature of life reveals the goodness of God, who surrounds us with evidence of that very goodness. Our call is to honor that goodness in one another, in ourselves, and in the whole of creation.

5 The petitioner asks for "living prayer." In other words, a prayer that is life, and life that is prayer. All aspects of living—speech, intention, understanding, doing—come within the encircling grace and presence of God. There is nothing outside the capacity of God's compassion and tenderness to transform and make new. As we become more faithful in prayer and more awakened to God's presence, we intentionally offer every aspect of our life, body and soul, to the Holy One who has breathed us into being, in whom we live, and who will receive us at the end of our earthly lives.

6 This Hebridean tradition keeps the creative tension of God's transcendent otherness ("compass my body about") and God's intimate presence within our hearts and souls. The prayer reminds us that both realities are ever true and ever present.

7 Encompassed by God's presence, we are also heirs of God's own life.

8 We are also made newly aware of the transitory nature of life. At every moment, all kinds of creatures are born in this world—human, animal, insect, bacterial. At every moment, all kinds of creatures are departing this world. A necessary awareness of "ties over-strict, ties over-dear" allows us to be mindful of our mortality.

From Thee It Came
Each thing I have received, from Thee it came,
Each thing for which I hope, from Thy love it will come,
Each thing I enjoy, it is of Thy bounty,
Each thing I ask, comes of Thy disposing.[4]

Holy God, loving Father, of the word everlasting,
Grant me to have of Thee this living prayer:
Lighten my understanding, kindle my will, begin my
    doing,[5]
Incite my love, strengthen my weakness, enfold my desire.
Cleanse my heart, make holy my soul, confirm my faith,
Keep safe my mind and compass my body about;
As I utter my prayer from my mouth,
In mine own heart may I feel Thy presence.[6]

And do Thou grant, O God of life,
That Thou be at my breast, that Thou be at my back,
That Thou give me my needs as may befit the crown
    Thou has promised to us in the world beyond.[7]

And grant Thou to me, Father beloved,
From Whom each thing that is freely flows,
That no tie over-strict, no tie over-dear
    May be between myself and this world below.[8]

The Carmina Gadelica, III, 59–61

9 The formula "bless to me" is found throughout the Hebridean prayers. It recalls the language of the Letter of Paul to the Ephesians, "Blessed be the God and Father of our Lord Jesus Christ, who has blessed us in Christ with every spiritual blessing in the heavenly places" (Ephesians 1:3). "Blessing" describes God's own life and vitality, and these prayers are a means of awakening to the blessing offered at every moment. In this petition, blessing is asked upon body and soul, belief and condition. In other words, blessing is asked upon the whole of life, singularly lived and uniquely experienced.

10 This prayer is offered at the time of dressing in the morning, that moment of clothing the body for the work of the day. As the body is newly covered, the prayer speaks a reminder of all that God's grace encompasses: heart, speech, and "the handling of my hand." Our hands are a means by which we connect to one another and to the world around us. Taking the time to recall what and who our hands touch, hold, and handle allows us to see and know how our lives are unfolding.

11 "The path of virtues" is a path of faith, hope, and love. This is a path, a way, a daily pilgrimage that we begin anew with each dawn. When we prepare for sleep, we recall the goodness we have known during the day, and the guidance God has given us for the day's walk in the path of virtues.

Prayer at Dressing
Bless to me, O God,
   My soul and my body;
Bless to me, O God,
My belief and my condition.[9]

Bless to me, O God,
   My heart and my speech,
And bless to me, O God,
   The handling of my hand.[10]

Strength and busyness of morning,
Habit and temper of modesty,
Force and wisdom of thought,
And Thine own path, O God of virtues,
   Till I go to sleep this night;

Thine own path, O God of virtues,
   Till I go to sleep this night.[11]

THE CARMINA GADELICA, III, 27

12 In the Outer Hebrides, fishing and herding were among the main means of livelihood in the nineteenth century, when Alexander Carmichael collected this prayer. This herding blessing leads us to see the relationship between the shepherd and the flock.

13 The shepherd's awareness of the dangers that await his sheep informs this petition for protection. In the rugged and rocky landscape of the Hebrides, even sure-footed sheep can lose their balance and fall into a pit.

14 The company of Mary, the Mother of Jesus, St. Brigit, and St. Michael the Archangel is named. The sheep and their shepherd travel in the community of saints—wooly flock and heavenly presences, all one company in the love of God.

15 The protection of three other saints is invoked. The company that travels with the herd is indeed numerous!

16 Nibbling, chewing, and munching, the herd is surrounded by the saintly companionship of angels, archangels, and the whole company of heaven. This is a vision of everyday work, hard work, done on earth, yet surrounded by heaven. There is no separation between this world and the heavenly realm; they are intricately, exquisitely bound to each other, for all is in God.

Herding Blessing

Closed to you be every pit,[12]
Smooth to you be every hill,
Snug to you be every bare spot,
Beside the cold mountains.[13]
The sanctuary of Mary Mother be yours,
The sanctuary of Brigit the loved be yours,
The sanctuary of Michael victorious be yours,[14]
Active and full be you gathered home.
The protection of shapely Cormac be yours,
The protection of Brendan of the ship be yours,
The protection of Maol Duinne the saint be yours[15]
In marshy ground and rocky ground.
The fellowship of Mary Mother be yours,
The fellowship of Brigit of kine be yours,
The fellowship of Michael victorious be yours,
In nibbling, in chewing, in munching.[16]

THE CARMINA GADELICA, IV, 41

17 Greeting the new day with gratefulness, this prayer also recalls the renewing of life in each cycle of day and night. Rising from rest, having received restoration in sleep, we rise with life itself, greeting the sun's first rays, which recall the glory of the uncreated light of God.

18 Shifting focus from the expansive horizon with the dawning light, the prayer moves to the distinctive reality of the petitioner. The great God of Life tends each person, body and soul. Echoing the psalmist, the prayer asks for the covering of God's protective presence, "the shadow of Thy wing" (Psalm 36:7).

19 Celtic spirituality holds fast to the essential goodness of humanity, body and soul. At the same time, there is a clarity with regard to sin, hurtful behaviors, and ill intent. The imagery of this last stanza depicts sin as an "ill haze"—something that distorts seeing and perception, yet also something that the strong wind of the Spirit can dissipate.

20 The risen life, the life of resurrection, is discovered daily in being raised "from the black." At a time when there was no electric light, the black of night would have been far darker than many of us experience today. The rising of the earthly body to the kindly light of the day—an everyday, ordinary experience—intimates the rising to new life that comes with death. Every day we are given an opportunity to practice, by being mindful, that we are "raised freely" to the kindly light.

21 These prayers from *The Carmina Gadelica* were prayed by a people who lived in harsh circumstances. Marked by storms and fierce wind, the climate of the Hebrides changes quickly. The rigorous demands of feeding and caring for a family in a subsistence economy were lived within a clear sense of life continually poured out on our behalf. Our every desire, sense, repute, thought, deed, way, and fame is the very locus of the life God freely pours upon the world.

Thanksgiving

Thanks to Thee, O God, that I have risen today,
    To the rising of this life itself;
May it be to Thine own glory, O God of every gift,
    And to the glory of my soul likewise.[17]

O great God, aid Thou my soul
    With the aiding of Thine own mercy;
Even as I clothe my body with wool,
    Cover Thou my soul with the shadow of Thy wing.[18]

Help me to avoid every sin,
    And the source of every sin to forsake;
And as the mist scatters on the crest of the hills,
    May each ill haze clear from my soul, O God.[19]

THE CARMINA GADELICA, III, 31

Gentle Christ

Thanks to Thee ever, O gentle Christ,
    That Thou hast raised me freely from the black
And from the darkness of last night
    To the kindly light of this day.[20]

Praise unto Thee, O God of all creatures,
    According to each life Thou has poured on me,
My desire, my word, my sense, my repute,
    My thought, my deed, my way, my fame.[21]

THE CARMINA GADELICA, III, 29

22   As we have seen in the previous selections, God's presence both surrounds us and indwells us. We are ever in God, and God is ever in us. Our task and our hope is that all that we express in thinking, speaking, creating, and acting is formed by that divine Presence.

23   As the Rev. Dr. William B. Green, professor of systematic theology has remarked with regard to Christian theology, "It's all in the prepositions" (Episcopal Seminary of the Southwest, lecture, 1982). This prayer startles us with the explicit invocation of God's own presence *in* all aspects of daily life. Our sleeping, our waking, our working, our watching, our waiting—all are infused with God's presence.

24   As we become more awake to this ever-present, ever-living God, we discover the continuity between life on earth, with the care of one another and the planet, and life in the world to come. Celtic spirituality perceives continuity where other spiritualities might perceive separation, sees connection where other spiritualities might see disconnection.

God to Enfold Me

God to enfold me,
    God to surround me,
God in my speaking,
    God in my thinking.[22]

God in my sleeping,
    God in my waking,
God in my watching,
    God in my hoping.

God in my life,
    God in my lips,
God in my soul,
    God in my heart.[23]

God in my sufficing,
    God in my slumber,
God in mine ever-living soul,
    God in mine eternity.[24]

The Carmina Gadelica, III, 53

25 This blessing, prayed as the mother of the household kindled the fire in the morning, gives us a sense of the pattern of the day in the Hebrides in the late nineteenth century. The woman of the household would have risen before dawn, in a house without electricity or heat. The kindling of the fire would be necessary to the preparation of food for her family, and for light and warmth. The kindling of the fire signaled the beginning of the day, the presence of the Source of the fire.

26 As she starts the fire, the mother calls on the Host of heaven, recognizing the near presence of angels, archangels, and the saints. She calls the archangels by name, and lives the spiritual reality of keeping house with "a great cloud of witnesses" (Hebrews 12:1).

27 The prayer expresses the Great Commandment, "You shall love the Lord your God with all your heart, and with all your soul, and with all your strength, and with all your mind; and your neighbor as yourself" (Luke 10:27, Deuteronomy 6:5, and Leviticus 19:18). Love of God directs us to love our neighbor.

28 We don't get to pick and choose whom God loves; the prayer specifically asks for aid in loving the foe, the knave, the thrall (that is, someone who is enslaved or controlled by another).

29 This kind of love is not sentimental or even emotional. This is the *agape* love of Jesus, expressed in acting for the good of others, remembering that every person is in God, whether or not his or her actions are consistent with that deep identity. It is also a love that tells the truth, knowing that honesty will be the ground of real relationship. The prayer that begins with the act of starting the fire moves to the web of relationships and includes the whole company of heaven.

Blessing of the Kindling

I will kindle my fire this morning[25]
In presence of the holy angels of heaven,
In presence of Ariel of the loveliest form,
In presence of Uriel of the myriad charms,
Without malice, without jealousy, without envy,
Without fear, without terror of any one under the sun,
But the Holy Son of God to shield me.
    Without malice, without jealousy, without envy,
    Without fear, without terror of any one under the sun,
    But the Holy Son of God to shield me.[26]

God, kindle Thou in my heart within
A flame of love to my neighbor,[27]
To my foe, to my friend, to my kindred all,
To the brave, to the knave, to the thrall,[28]
O Son of the loveliest Mary,
From the lowliest thing that liveth,
To the Name that is highest of all,
    O Son of the loveliest Mary,
    From the lowliest thing that liveth,
    To the Name that is highest of all.[29]

THE CARMINA GADELICA, I, 231

30 Our work is offered in partnership with God; our work is a co-creative endeavor. The milkmaid recognizes God's presence in the little cow, in her desire to draw milk from the udder, in the "handling of her hands."

31 In our everyday work and activities, God is present in the work, and in the handling of our hands.

32 The prayer also demonstrates a reverence for the embodied interaction of cow and milkmaid, teats and fingers. Celtic spirituality is not afraid of the embodied presence of God in and through all that God has brought forth. The cow is a sign of God's love and creativity. The milkmaid's prayer celebrates this animal and her relationship to it, as well as the bounty of the milk. The prayer reminds us to celebrate the ways in which God's goodness and blessing is known in our ordinary encounters, those moments when reverence and delight reveal the daily gift of God.

33 The day begins and ends with an awareness of God's presence. This prayer, said upon preparing for sleep, invites us to the startling truth that we are "lying down" in the presence of God, Christ, and the Spirit. The tradition speaks of the "Three that seek my heart" (*The Carmina Gadelica*, III, 33), a tender way of addressing God as Trinity. God, Christ, and the Spirit dwell within the home. The "Three that seek my heart" are also mysteriously One in the Love and Action.

Milking Prayer
Bless, O God, my little cow,
    Bless, O God, my desire;
Bless Thou my partnership
    And the milking of my hands, O God.[30]

Bless, O God, each teat,
    Bless, O God, each finger;[31]
Bless Thou each drop
    That goes into my pitcher, O God![32]

THE CARMINA GADELICA, IV, 65

Night Prayer
I lie down this night with God,
    And God will lie down with me;
I lie down this night with Christ,
    And Christ will lie down with me;
I lie down this night with Spirit,
    And the Spirit will lie down with me;
God and Christ and the Spirit
    Be lying down with me.[33]

THE CARMINA GADELICA, III, 333

34 Euros Bowen, an Anglican Welsh priest, offers a contemporary example of the Celtic emphasis on the sacredness of the ordinary and the everyday. His prayer-poem begins with a description of a refrigerator full of food. As he beholds the food, he remembers its origin.

35 The seeds nurtured in the darkness of soil, warmed by sun and moistened by rain, have been a symbol of the risen life of Christ since the time of St. Paul. (See, for example, 1 Corinthians 15:36–38.) As Bowen reflects on the contents of his refrigerator, he is led to reflect on the life of the seed and the power of God's Light to bring forth new life.

A Refrigerator
A cupboard
and buttress of technology
in the kitchen,
a very material and useful
refuge:
keeping together
the mild of meadows,
the pasture's honey,
the produce of fields and forests,
the goodness
of the cream and the mill,
the generosity
of the wine vat.[34]

All that was conceived
by the air
and the earth
in the graves of the soil
and that was nurtured
by water
and fire
in the cradle of the earth
is born anew:[35]

(continued on page 101)

36   "Anamnesis" literally means "to be against forgetting," "to remember." The refrigerator, humming away in the kitchen of an ordinary Welsh house, leads the poet to remember God's gift and blessing shown to us in every kind of food, every meal, every refrigerator. And we are made mindful of the intimate relationship we have with the earth, this planet of God's own making.

The trout's resurrection
beside the descents of the valley,
the salmon's leap
by the falls of the weir,
the firmament's power
gladdens

the slopes of the lemon,
breezes
sweetening the juice of oranges.

This is the culture of the sun's galleries
and the utterance of the rain's pastures:

The store cupboard
of the anamnesis
of the images of earth.[36]

EUROS BOWEN, TWENTIETH-CENTURY POET
AND ANGLICAN PRIEST, WALES

5 □ Soul Friends

The Celtic Christians were clear that walking a path of faith is well nigh impossible without a true friend and companion. In the Gospel of John, Jesus tells the disciples, "You are my friends if you do what I command you" (John 15:14). He has just commanded them to love one another as he has loved them. Following this stunning invitation from Jesus in the Gospel of John, the Celtic church encouraged this relationship formed in Christ.

Soul friendship is distinctive because it is marked by this kind of love—a love centered in prayer and joy, in sharing the bread of life in its various forms and in mutual disclosure. In the early Celtic churches, the practice of soul friendship was one of mutual encouragement, confession, and penance. A soul friend is a person who will allow you to tell the whole truth of yourself, and encourage you to seek healing and restoration. A soul friend also has the fine gift of being able to share in joy, a gift that our highly competitive culture does not call forth.

The late John O'Donohue, twentieth-century Irish author and poet, noted that the Celtic Christians were distinctive in recognizing that friendship is a creative and subversive force. A soul friend will be a hearth where we may sit in silence and be warmed. A soul friend will be a place of belonging and rest. And a soul friend will help kindle the divine fire within the soul.

Ultimately, Jesus is our dearest soul friend. We know his presence in and through those who walk with us in our spiritual life. We come to trust this friendship extended by God through Jesus.

This way of living and being with one another, of being humble enough to readily seek correction and guidance from a friendly presence, characterizes the Celtic spiritual life at its core. Jesus is the one who walks with us, guides us, shares his own life with us, and receives us at the time of our earthly death.

1 St. Brigid of Kildare, also known as St. Brigit and St. Ffraid (in Wales), was renowned for her strong words about soul friendship. The Irish *anam cara* and the Welsh *periglour* both mean "soul friend," a particular way of befriending that intentionally honors and nurtures the life of the soul. In Celtic Christian tradition, a soul friend is so essential that not having one is like not having a head! In other words, without a soul friend, you cannot rightly see, hear, perceive, discern, discover, or know. Without a soul friend you cannot tell whether a context "smells" wrong. You cannot "taste" goodness. You will stumble along, creating habits of thinking and behaving that could become destructive. You cannot walk a spiritual path alone.

2 Pelagius understands the human person to be made in the image and likeness of God (see Genesis 1:26). While Pelagius is quite clear about the destructive and violent behaviors that tear apart human community and ruin lives, he is also insistent that our deepest identity is inviolate. Our deepest identity is found in the capacity to follow Jesus in our daily lives, a capacity that comes from God, who in Jesus claims us as God's own.

3 Pelagius insists that we need companions in the Way, soul friends who will guide us along right pathways and help us recognize our God-given capacity to live compassionately and generously. Trying to live in this way without a soul friend is foolhardy.

4 Pelagius's letter to Demetrias, a "woman who has kept herself a virgin for the sake of Christ," is notable because it is addressed to a woman. Celtic Christian spirituality, from its inception and following the example of Jesus, accords women the freedom to choose a sacred path. Celtic culture in Ireland and Wales was characterized by women being able to own land, sue for divorce, and become educated as lawyers and physicians. When the gospel came to those areas, women became strong leaders and advocates of the Christian faith, equal to men. There is evidence that women were functioning in priestly ways, presiding at celebrations of Holy Communion.

A person without a soul friend is like a body without a
head.[1]

ATTRIBUTED TO ST. BRIGID OF KILDARE

Whenever I give moral instruction, I first try to demonstrate
the inherent power and quality of human nature. I try to
show the wonderful virtues which all human beings can
acquire. Most people look at the virtues in others, and
imagine that such virtues are far beyond their reach. Yet
God has implanted in every person the capacity to attain
the very highest level of virtue.[2] But people cannot grow in
virtue on their own. We each need companions to guide
and direct us on the way of righteousness; without such
companions we are liable to stray from the firm path, and
then sink into the mud of despair. At first a companion who
has achieved a high level of virtue can seem utterly
different from oneself. But as friendship grows, one begins
to see in the companion a mirror of oneself.[3]

PELAGIUS, *LETTER TO DEMETRIAS*[4]

5 Celtic Christianity is distinctive in this insistence on soul friendship. With a soul friend, true vulnerability is possible because this friend wills all good and all blessing for us, even when—especially when—we are in error and stand in need of correction. A soul friend will not shy away from speaking the truth in love. When counsel is offered with true kindness, we are able to receive the strong medicine of truth—words that both offer renewal and restoration and honor God's light and life already present within us.

Indeed we each need one special friend, who may be called a friend of the soul. We must open our souls completely to this friend, hiding nothing and revealing everything. And we must allow this friend to assess and judge what he sees.[5]

PELAGIUS, LETTER TO DEMETRIAS

6 □ Pilgrimage

In the first years after Jesus' death and resurrection, what was to become "Christianity" was known as "the Way." (See Acts of the Apostles 9:2.) Those who were followers of Jesus walked in his spiritual path. These early members of the Way made this pilgrimage as a company.

When the gospel first came to Britain and Ireland, those countries were characterized by rural tribal communities. Although there were Roman roads in the eastern part of Britain, Wales remained a place of footpaths and rugged terrain. To go from one small community to another, people often walked. The prayers we have received, as well as the lives of the saints, offer a glimpse of a people invoking God while on the move.

We find in the Celtic Christians a distinctive phenomenon: the wandering saints. These were men and women who journeyed "for the love of Christ."[1] They set forth without a particular destination in mind, walking from one place to another, following the promptings of the Holy Spirit. They also gave us a model of pilgrimage on water, a model that tends to give us pause. Using a small round boat with no oars (called a coracle or a curragh), a pilgrim band would climb into the boat, cast off, and entrust themselves to "the currents of divine love." Eventually, either the sea or the river would bring them to rest at a place they had not chosen, for they allowed themselves to be completely open to the movement of the water. That place would be known as "the place of my resurrection," for they would have been led to that place by the Holy Spirit, and would probably die there (unless prompted to make another sea pilgrimage).

This way of pilgrimage demonstrates stunning trust in God's guidance and an ability to let go of expectation and outcome. When we "get into the coracle" and see "the place of my resurrection," we hold each day as a gift from God, and wait for guidance as the day unfolds.

1 Each step along the pilgrimage of life is taken in the company of God, Jesus, and Spirit, the Three of my love. The Trinity, in whom we live and move and have our being, is with us no matter the twists and turns, the difficulties and joys of our lives.

2 Each landscape of our lives is known to God; each terrain that we encounter is the very dwelling place of God.

God Be with Thee

God be with thee in every pass,
Jesus be with thee on every hill,
Spirit be with thee on every stream,
Headland and ridge and lawn;[1]

Each sea and land, each moor and meadow,
Each lying down, each rising up,
In the trough of the waves, on the crest of the billows,
Each step of the journey thou goest.[2]

THE CARMINA GADELICA, III, 195

3 As we walk our life path, praying this prayer invokes God's presence in the very earth upon which we step. We recognize that God is with us in the place our feet touch, no matter where we walk, no matter where we are led.

4 As we make our way, we ask God's blessing on our intentions, on our heart's desire, on our deepest hope. We have the humility to ask God's guidance in discerning well as we live our intentions, our loves, our hopes. Lastly, we recognize that our own gaze, if it is loving and steady, will be a blessing to others. When we ask God to bless our eyes, our sight, we ask to see as God sees.

The Earth Beneath My Foot

Bless to me, O God,
The earth beneath my foot.
Bless to me, O God,
The path whereon I go;
Bless to me, O God,
The thing of my desire;
Thou ever more of evermore,
Bless Thou to me my rest.[3]

Bless to me the thing
Whereon is set my mind,
Bless to me the thing
Whereon is set my love;
Bless to me the thing
Whereon is set my hope;
O Thou King of Kings!
Bless Thou to me mine eye![4]

THE CARMINA GADELICA, III, 181

5 This journey prayer invokes God's protection and active aid. The "two hands" of God are the Son, Jesus, and the Spirit.

6 This second stanza invokes God's shielding presence, which recalls St. Paul's language of the "armor of God" (see Ephesians 5:10–17). In addition, a tender sense of God keeping us and bathing us evokes a maternal image. This is a robust sense of God-with-us, extending care, protection, nurture, and shielding.

7 God is both our destination and our path, and God is both our companion and our guide. Celtic spirituality affirms the truth of both, and encourages us to remember that there is no place, no time, where God is not present. God will also greet us at the end of our journey.

8 In the course of a life, in the walking of a spiritual path, there will be times when we feel lost or confused, abandoned or betrayed. This prayer affirms God's strength and constancy, no matter the circumstances we may encounter.

May God Make Safe
May God make safe to you each steep,
May God make open to you each pass,
May God make clear to you each road,
And may He take you in the clasp
Of His own two hands.[5]

May God shield you on every steep,
May Christ keep you in every path,
May Spirit bathe you in every pass.[6]

THE CARMINA GADELICA, III, 203

Pilgrimage
Who to Rome goes
Much labour, little profit knows;
For God, on earth though long you've sought him,
You'll miss at Rome unless you've brought him.[7]

SEDULIUS IN CODEX BOERNERIANUS, NINTH CENTURY, IRISH

Thou Dost Not Fall
As the rain hides the stars, as the autumn mist hides the
hills, as the clouds veil the blue of the sky, so the dark
happenings of my lot hide the shining of thy face from me.
Yet, if I may hold thy hand in the darkness, it is enough.
Since I know that, though I may stumble in my going, thou
dost not fall.[8]

TRADITIONAL GAELIC, TRANSLATED BY ALISTAIR MACLEAN

7 □ Social Justice

The emphatic embrace of the Incarnation leads Celtic saints, poets, theologians, and missionaries to strongly voice the social import of the gospel. In these excerpts from writings by Saint Patrick, Pelagius, and the Welsh poet David James Jones (Gwennalt), the sacred nature of the human person is confirmed and the social and communal responsibilities of the Christian community become clear and irreducible. Christians are given the task and the responsibility to be agents of transformation in society, so that goods are distributed equitably, any kind of slavery is eradicated, and all people are treated with equal respect. Christian communities are to emulate the particular attention that Jesus gives to the outcast, the poor, the hungry, the sick, and the prisoners and captives. There is no separation of holy versus unholy. This is a perspective on our life together shaped by profoundly knowing that "in Christ all things hold together" (Colossians 1:17b).

That vision has a distinctive moral rigor about it, and leads all members of the Christian community to reflect upon their own actions in the world, their own investments. Each person who follows in this Way, in the company of soul friends, is called to a critique of the society in which we live and to ongoing humility, conversion, and transformation for the life of the world.

1 The "valley of dry bones" is a reference to Ezekiel 37, in which the prophet has a vision of a valley full of bones, a reference to wasting and death. When a society is characterized by greed, envy, malice, and lack of care, a kind of spiritual death transpires.

2 Pelagius recognizes that we know what it is to hate. He invites us to name that experience, and to allow God to transform it through action. We learn to "walk the talk," so to speak. We begin to be formed by acting in a compassionate way, training body, mind, and spirit. To refrain from acting maliciously is only the first step. The second step in creating a just and peaceful society is then to *act* in a generous way toward the very persons you might have chosen to ignore or hurt.

A society in which people only avoided certain actions, but never did anything good, would be utterly dead; it would be like the valley of dry bones which the prophet describes.[1] A society can only live if people love and serve one another. So when you are aware of hatred in your heart, do not simply suppress it, but transform it into love. When you desire to commit a malicious act, do not simply stop yourself; transform that act into a generous one.[2]

PELAGIUS, LETTER TO CELANTIA

3 Patrick so rejects the practice of slavery that he calls for Coroticus and his soldiers to make reparations and do penance. Patrick understands that slavery rends the fabric of a just society, turning human beings into commodities. He affirms the sacred nature of each person, and demands that each person be treated with dignity and respect.

4 Saint Patrick (b. around 390), whom we know as the patron saint of Ireland, began his life there as a slave. In his autobiography, Patrick tells the reader that as an adolescent, he was kidnapped and taken to Ireland against his will. After six years of being enslaved, Patrick had a dream in which he was told that a ship would be waiting for him. He walked for miles and managed to escape. Years later, he had a dream in which he was called back to Ireland to serve the very people who had enslaved him. He followed the vision from the dream, returning as a bishop of the Christian church. His own experience of slavery led him to be fiercely against this practice, and to speak out against those who perpetuated it.

The *Letter to Coroticus* is addressed to an Irish chieftain who had taken some of Patrick's converts into slavery. When Coroticus failed to respond to a plea to set the captives free, Patrick responded by excommunicating Coroticus. He firmly believed that one could not be a Christian and have slaves. For his day and time, this was a radical interpretation of the good news of Jesus. Slavery was not illegal in many Western countries until the latter half of the nineteenth century, despite the fact that those countries were predominantly Christian.

5 The suffering of women slaves moved Patrick deeply; he remarked on their courage and their tenacity. Patrick's life exemplifies St. Paul's understanding of life in Christ: "There is no longer Jew or Greek, there is no longer slave or free, there is no longer male and female; for all of you are one in Christ Jesus" (Galatians 3:28).

6 Patrick also wrote *Confession*, in which he tells of his life, his prayers, and his desire to serve God. Following the example of Jesus, Patrick confirms the dignity of women. Slavery in and of itself is horrific.

Wherefore, then I plead with you earnestly, ye holy and humble of heart, it is not permissible to court the favour of such people, nor to take food or drink with them, not even to accept their alms, until they make reparation to God in hardships, through penance, with shedding of tears, and set free the baptized servants of God and handmaids of Christ, for whom He died and was crucified.[3]

SAINT PATRICK, LETTER TO COROTICUS[4]

But the greatest is the suffering of those women who live in slavery. All the time they have to endure terror and threats. But the Lord gave His grace to many of His maidens; for, though they are forbidden to do so, many of them follow Him bravely.[5]

SAINT PATRICK, CONFESSION[6]

7 Patrick knows that actions reveal our heart's intent. In the actions of Coroticus and his soldiers, men who profess to follow the way of Jesus, Patrick sees criminal action that is completely inconsistent with the way of faith, hope, and love. Patrick and Pelagius both insist that our actions reveal the intention of our hearts and souls. Justice will be possible only as communities hold one another accountable when injustice occurs.

8 Pelagius was not welcome in Rome because of his scathing critique of the opulence of the clergy and the pope. He took to heart the words from Matthew 25:34–36: "Come, you that are blessed by my Father, inherit the kingdom prepared for you from the foundation of the world; for I was hungry and you gave me food, I was thirsty and you gave me something to drink, I was a stranger and you welcomed me, I was naked and you gave me clothing, I was sick and you took care of me, I was in prison and you visited me." In his clear, insistent prose, Pelagius calls us to act in ways that honor and remember the presence of Christ in all persons, even those who are our enemies and persecutors.

Where, then, will Coroticus with his criminals, rebels against Christ, where will they see themselves, they who distribute baptized women as prizes—for a miserable temporal kingdom, which will pass away in a moment? As a cloud or smoke that is dispersed by the wind, so shall the deceitful wicked perish at the presence of the Lord; but the just shall feast with great constancy with Christ; they shall judge nations, and rule over wicked kings for ever and ever. Amen.[7]

SAINT PATRICK, *LETTER TO COROTICUS*

How can you call yourself a Christian since you do not act like one? "Christian" is the name of justice, goodness, integrity, patience, chastity, prudence, humility, humanity, innocence, and true religion. How can you claim this for yourself when you possess only a few of so many virtues? That person is a Christian who is so not only in name but also in deed; who imitates and follows Christ in all things; who is holy, innocent, and pure; who is uncorrupted; in whose heart there is no place for evil; in whose heart there is only true religion and goodness; who is incapable of hurting or wounding anyone, but can only come to the aid of everyone. That person is a Christian who, with Christ as an example, cannot even hate their enemies but does good to those who oppose them, praying for their persecutors and enemies.[8]

PELAGIUS, *ON THE CHRISTIAN LIFE*

9 Pelagius understands that the danger of wealth is not the wealth itself, but the isolating effect it may have on the one who holds the riches. It is easy to forget what it is like to be hungry, homeless, thirsty, or naked when we never have to worry about the next meal, our child's health, or having adequate housing. Reflecting on the book of Exodus from the Hebrew Scriptures, Pelagius remarks that the fact of being enslaved in Egypt and wandering for forty years in the desert gave the Israelites an acute awareness of the plight of others. The Christian life is an invitation to nurture that awareness and be ready to serve the sick, the hungry, the homeless, those in prison, the poor, the refugees—all who are on the margins of society.

I do not think that it was without reason or without the Providence of God that he determined that they [the Jewish people] should live in a deserted place, making them leave their homeland and journey to a foreign land, that is, to Egypt.... For no one is more ready to pity the exile or the stranger than someone who knows the effects of exile. No one offers lodging to a homeless guest so much as someone who has themselves been dependent on the generosity of others. No one is more likely to feed the hungry or to give a drink to the thirsty than someone who has themselves suffered hunger and thirst. No one is so ready to cover the naked with their own clothes than someone who knows the pain of nakedness and cold. No one is more likely to come to the aid of people who face troubles, misery, and hardship than those who have themselves experienced the misfortune of troubles, misery, and hardship.[9]

PELAGIUS, *ON THE CHRISTIAN LIFE*

10 Pelagius was held in contempt and charged with heresy. It seems incomprehensible that his writings could have been construed to be against the teachings of Jesus. He firmly, almost stridently, insists on the radical nature of following Jesus. He tells his readers to hold their lives lightly, to be willing to honor God in all places and at all times, even when that results in being scorned by society. He sides with those who are without political and economic power.

That person is a Christian who is merciful to all, who is not
motivated by injustice, who cannot endure the oppression
of the poor before their very eyes, who comes to the aid of
the wretched, who helps the needy, who mourns with those
who mourn, who feels the suffering of others as if it were
their own, who is moved to tears by the tears of others,
whose house is open to all, whose doors are closed to none,
whose table is familiar to all the poor, whose food is offered
to all, whose goodness is known to all, and at whose hands
no one suffers injustice, who serves God day and night,
who ceaselessly considers and meditates upon his
commandments, who makes themselves poor in the world
that they may be rich in God, who is without honor in
society that they may appear glorified before God and his
angels, who seems to have nothing false or untrue in their
heart, whose soul is simple and unstained, whose
conscience is faithful and pure, whose mind is wholly in
God, whose hope is all in Christ, who desires the things of
heaven rather than the things of earth, who leaves behind
human things that they may have the things of God.[10]

PELAGIUS, *ON THE CHRISTIAN LIFE*

11 This "rune," or poem pointing to mystery, declares the mysterious presence of Christ in the stranger. It is worth noting that the stranger is seen rather than overlooked or ignored.

12 The response to seeing the stranger is one of hospitality for body, mind, and spirit. Food and drink are supplied so that the body's needs may be met. Music is offered for the soothing of a weary spirit and the opportunity for resting in beauty.

13 The offerings are made in the name of the Triune God, the Holy One who is Father, Son, and Holy Spirit.

14 The stranger's response to this kind hospitality is to bless the host of the feast with an encompassing blessing for the giver, the household, the land, and the creatures. All come within the ample blessing of this mysterious stranger.

15 The lark knows the true identity of the stranger, and the lark's song is heard, understood, and interpreted. The book of creation encourages us to be on the lookout for the strangers in our midst, to develop eyes to see and ears to hear, so that we too may prepare a feast for those in need. The motive for social justice is far deeper than wanting to further a cause or do the right thing. Social justice is rooted and grounded in the reality of the love that allows Jesus to guide us in perceiving his presence in the whole human family.

Gaelic Rune of Hospitality

I saw a stranger yestreen,[11]
I put food in the eating place,
Drink in the drinking place,
Music in the listening place,[12]
And in the sacred name of the Triune,[13]
He blessed myself and my house,
My cattle and my dear ones,[14]
And the lark said in her song
Often, often, often
Goes the Christ in the stranger's guise.[15]

TRADITIONAL GAELIC
(ORAL TRADITION, QUOTED BY RONALD FERGUSON,
CHASING THE WILD GOOSE: THE STORY OF THE IONA COMMUNITY
[GLASGOW: WILD GOOSE PUBLICATIONS, 1998], PAGE 25)

16 David James Jones, or Gwennalt (his bardic name), was a Welsh poet of the twentieth century. His poem speaks to the experience of "thin places," and reminds us that the Holy Spirit is the giver of those experiences. In these verses, Gwennalt leads the reader to see the connection between perceiving the sacred created nature of the universe, which includes the sacred nature of each creature and each human being. This short poem reminds us that each worker is a sacred being. If we begin to see the universe as God's creation, we are eventually led to question the ways in which workers are not treated as persons. We begin to reflect on and question social and political structures that do not respect the life of every human being.

The Creation

When the Spirit makes thin the canvas we see that the
 universe is a creation,
That the worker, because he is a child of God, is a person,
And we see The Christ rising from his Cross and Grave like
 the glory of
The sun in the ailing snow to light up the seventh
 Heaven.[16]

GWENNALT (DAVID JAMES JONES), TWENTIETH-CENTURY POET, WALES

8 □ Blessing as a Way of Life

Throughout the writings and prayers that we receive from the Celtic Christian tradition, life is known as a blessing and a gift. We come from the Holy One, whose essence is infinite goodness. Out of that goodness, we have come forth. In our daily lives, we are surrounded by that goodness. In our deepest soul, that goodness dwells within us, inseparably tying us to the God we know in Jesus. The blessing we receive is an eternal reality. It is not a matter of quantifiable possessions or material wealth. This is the blessing of our very being, of our true identity.

What is it to walk in blessing? The Celtic pilgrims show us that when we walk in blessing, we are living in a growing awareness of God's presence and mercy, extended to us with infinite wisdom and grace, because of who God is. We bless God by becoming aware of God's mercies and goodness to us, receiving that mercy and goodness, and allowing our lives to be transformed into active blessing of others. We become more generous and more compassionate, as persons and as communities. We seek the burnishing of the radiant divine image within us, and we humbly invite God's guidance and correction that we may grow in the likeness of God, so that the whole world may be charged with compassion, truth, and kindness.

1 The blessing of God, the God of grace, is with us at every moment, whether we are awake or asleep. The blessing of God—that pouring out of God's own Light and life—brings us into being, sustains us, and makes us new. We are recipients of the blessing and we are called to live lives that bless others and the creation, "the earth that is beneath my sole."

2 The blessing of God is always the blessing of God, the risen Jesus, and Spirit, ever present, inseparably united as the Holy One in whom we dwell, in whom we rise, and in whom we lie down.

Journey Prayer
God, bless to me this day,
    God, bless to me this night;
Bless, O bless, Thou God of grace,
    Each day and hour of my life;
Bless, O bless, Thou God of grace,
    Each day and hour of my life.

God, bless the pathway on which I go,
    God, bless the earth that is beneath my sole;
    Bless, O God, and give to me Thy love,
O God of gods, bless my rest and my repose;
    Bless, O God, and give to me Thy love,
And bless, O God of gods, my repose.[1]

THE CARMINA GADELICA, III, 179

And Well May It Befall You
God's blessing be yours,
And well may it befall you;
Christ's blessing be yours,
And well be you entreated;
Spirit's blessing be yours,
And well spend you your lives,
    Each day that you rise up,
    Each night that you lie down.[2]

THE CARMINA GADELICA, III, 211

3 We are ever within the presence of the Holy One, the great God whose two hands are the Son, Jesus, and the Holy Spirit. We are aided by God's kindness and goodness, in all aspects of our lives.

4 In this contemporary blessing written by the late John O'Donohue, Irish author and poet, we are offered a deep trust in the working of God within us, healing and renewing, birthing and transforming, tending all that needs blessing. We are led toward a remarkable hope that nothing is beyond God's mercy, nothing is beyond the kindness of God's care. The places of despair, bitterness, fear, and desperation that exist within us are also ever within the presence of God. God's tender yearning that all be made well endures through all time and in all places.

The Guarding of the Trinity

The guarding of the God of life be on you,
The guarding of loving Christ be on you,
The guarding of Holy Spirit be on you
    Every night of your lives,
To aid you and enfold you
    Each day and night of your lives.[3]

THE CARMINA GADELICA, III, 207

To Come Home to Yourself

May all that is unforgiven in you
Be released.

May your fears yield
Their deepest tranquilities.

May all that is unlived in you
Blossom into a future
Graced with love.[4]

JOHN O'DONOHUE, TWENTY-FIRST CENTURY
POET AND WRITER, IRELAND

5 The rhythms of the tide, the waxing and waning of the moon, the rising and setting of the sun—all these natural rhythms are part of God's design. Our own lives have an ebb and a flow, too, and as we discover the blessing and presence of God within that ebb and flow, we are more deeply formed by the Love that speaks everything into being.

The Ebb and the Flow

As it was,
As it is,
As it shall be
Evermore,
O Thou Triune of Grace!
With the ebb,
With the flow,
O Thou Triune of Grace!
With the ebb,
With the flow.[5]

THE CARMINA GADELICA, II, 217

☐ Notes

Introduction

1. *Threshold of Light* has been published in the United States as *Daily Readings in Prayer and Praise in the Celtic Tradition*, ed. A. M. Allchin and Esther de Waal (Springfield, IL: Templegate, 1987).

2. See *Pseudo-Dionysius: The Complete Works*, trans. and ed. Paul Rorem (Mahwah, NJ: Paulist Press, 1987).

3. See Lars Thunberg, *Microcosm and Mediator: The Theological Anthropology of Maximus the Confessor* (Chicago: Open Court, 1995).

4. *Julian of Norwich: Showings*, trans. Edmund Colledge and James Walsh (Mahwah, NJ: Paulist Press, 1977).

5. See, for example, Kallistos Ware, *The Orthodox Way*, rev. ed. (Yonkers, NY: St. Vladimir's Press, 1995).

6. See Mary C. Earle, *The Desert Mothers: Spiritual Practices from the Women of the Wilderness* (Harrisburg, PA: Morehouse, 2007); Roberta Bondi, *To Love as God Loves* (Philadelphia: Fortress Press, 1987); John Chryssavgis, *In the Heart of the Desert* (Bloomington, IN: World Wisdom, 2007); Henri M. Nouwen, *The Way of the Heart* (New York: Ballantine Books, 2003).

7. See *The Carmina Gadelica: Hymns and Incantations*, trans. and ed. Alexander Carmichael (Hudson, NY: Lindisfarne Press, 1992), pp. 630–31.

6. Pilgrimage

1. See, e.g., Esther de Waal, *The Celtic Way of Prayer* (New York: Doubleday, 1997), and Helen Waddell, *The Wandering Scholars* (Ann Arbor: University of Michigan Press, 1989).

Suggestions for Further Reading □

Allchin, A. M. *God's Presence Makes the World: The Celtic Vision through the Centuries in Wales.* London: Darton, Longman and Todd, Ltd., 1997.

———. *Praise Above All: Discovering the Welsh Tradition.* Cardiff: University of Wales Press, 1991.

Allchin, A. M., and Esther de Waal. *Daily Readings in Prayer and Praise in the Celtic Tradition.* Springfield, IL: Templegate, 1987.

Carmichael, Alexander. *The Carmina Gadelica: Hymns and Incantations.* Hudson, NY: Lindisfarne Press, 1992.

Davies, Oliver, trans. and ed. *Celtic Spirituality.* New York: Paulist Press, 1999.

Davies, Oliver, and Fiona Bowie. *Celtic Christian Spirituality: An Anthology of Medieval and Modern Sources.* New York: Continuum, 1995.

De Waal, Esther. *The Celtic Way of Prayer: The Recovery of the Religious Imagination.* New York: Doubleday, 1997.

———. *Every Earthly Blessing: Rediscovering the Celtic Tradition.* Ann Arbor, MI: Servant Publications, 1991.

Earle, Mary C., and Sylvia Maddox. *Holy Companions: Spiritual Practices from the Celtic Saints.* Harrisburg, PA: Morehouse, 2004.

Flower, Robin. *The Irish Tradition.* Dublin: Lilliput Press, 1994.

Joyce, Timothy. *Celtic Christianity: A Sacred Tradition, a Vision of Hope.* Maryknoll, NY: Orbis Books, 1998.

———. *A Retreat with Patrick: Discovering God in All.* Cincinnati: Saint Anthony Messenger Press, 2000.

Mackey, James P. *An Introduction to Celtic Christianity.* Edinburgh: T & T Clark, 1989.

MacLeod, George F. *The Whole Earth Shall Cry Glory.* Glasgow: Wild Goose Publications, 1985.

Newell, J. Philip. *The Book of Creation: An Introduction to Celtic Spirituality.* New York: Paulist Press, 1999.

———. *Celtic Benediction: Morning and Night Prayer.* Grand Rapids, MI: William B. Eerdmans, 2000.

———. *Celtic Treasure: Daily Scriptures and Prayers.* Grand Rapids, MI: William B. Eerdmans, 2005.

————. *Listening for the Heartbeat of God: A Celtic Spirituality.* New York: Paulist Press, 1997.

O'Donoghue, Noel Dermot. *The Mountain Behind the Mountain: Aspects of the Celtic Tradition.* Edinburgh: T & T Clark, 1993.

O'Donohue, John. *Anam Cara: A Book of Celtic Wisdom.* New York: Harper-Collins, 1998.

————. *To Bless the Space Between Us: A Book of Blessings.* New York: Doubleday, 2008.

O'Loughlin, Thomas. *Journeys on the Edges: The Celtic Tradition.* Maryknoll, NY: Orbis, 2000.

O'Malley, Brendan. *Celtic Blessings and Prayers: Making All Things Sacred.* Mystic, CT: Twenty-Third Publications, 1998.

————. *A Celtic Primer: The Complete Celtic Worship Resource and Collection.* Harrisburg, PA: Morehouse, 2002.

————. *A Welsh Pilgrim's Manual/Cydymaith y Pererin.* Llandysul, Dyfed, Wales: Gomer Press, 1989.

Sheldrake, Philip. *Living Between Worlds: Place and Journey in Celtic Spirituality.* Lanham, MD: Cowley Publications, 1996.

Van de Weyer, Robert, ed. *The Letters of Pelagius: Celtic Soul Friend.* Evesham, UK: Arthur James, Ltd., 1995.

Credits □

Notes □

☐ Notes

Notes ☐

Notes

Inspiration

Deepening Engagement
Essential Wisdom for Listening and Leading with Purpose, Meaning and Joy
By Diane M. Millis, PhD; Foreword by Rob Lehman
A toolkit for community building as well as a resource for personal growth and small group enrichment.
5 x 7¼, 176 pp, Quality PB, 978-1-59473-584-4 **$14.99**

The Rebirthing of God
Christianity's Struggle for New Beginnings
By John Philip Newell
Drawing on modern prophets from East and West, and using the holy island of Iona as an icon of new beginnings, Celtic poet, peacemaker and scholar John Philip Newell dares us to imagine a new birth from deep within Christianity, a fresh stirring of the Spirit.
6 x 9, 160 pp, HC, 978-1-59473-542-4 **$19.99**

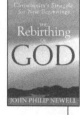

Finding God Beyond Religion: A Guide for Skeptics, Agnostics & Unorthodox Believers Inside & Outside the Church
By Tom Stella; Foreword by The Rev. Canon Marianne Wells Borg
Reinterprets traditional religious teachings central to the Christian faith for people who have outgrown the beliefs and devotional practices that once made sense to them.
6 x 9, 160 pp, Quality PB, 978-1-59473-485-4 **$16.99**

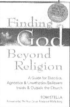

Fully Awake and Truly Alive: Spiritual Practices to Nurture Your Soul
By Rev. Jane E. Vennard; Foreword by Rami Shapiro
Illustrates the joys and frustrations of spiritual practice, offers insights from various religious traditions and provides exercises and meditations to help us become more fully alive.
6 x 9, 208 pp, Quality PB, 978-1-59473-473-1 **$16.99**

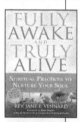

Perennial Wisdom for the Spiritually Independent
Sacred Teachings—Annotated & Explained
Annotation by Rami Shapiro; Foreword by Richard Rohr
Weaves sacred texts and teachings from the world's major religions into a coherent exploration of the five core questions at the heart of every religion's search.
5½ x 8½, 336 pp, Quality PB, 978-1-59473-515-8 **$16.99**

Journeys of Simplicity: Traveling Light with Thomas Merton, Bashō Edward Abbey, Annie Dillard & Others By Philip Harnden
5 x 7¼, 144 pp, Quality PB, 978-1-59473-181-5 **$12.99**

Saving Civility: 52 Ways to Tame Rude, Crude & Attitude for a Polite Planet
By Sara Hacala 6 x 9, 240 pp, Quality PB, 978-1-59473-314-7 **$16.99**

Spiritually Healthy Divorce: Navigating Disruption with Insight & Hope
By Carolyne Call 6 x 9, 224 pp, Quality PB, 978-1-59473-288-1 **$16.99**

Or phone, mail or email to: SKY LIGHT PATHS Publishing
An imprint of Turner Publishing Company
4507 Charlotte Avenue • Suite 100 • Nashville, Tennessee 37209
Tel: (615) 255-2665 • www.skylightpaths.com
Prices subject to change.

Sacred Texts—SkyLight Illuminations Series

Offers today's spiritual seeker an enjoyable entry into the great classic texts of the world's spiritual traditions. Each classic is presented in an accessible translation, with facing pages of guided commentary from experts, giving you the keys you need to understand the history, context and meaning of the text.

CHRISTIANITY

The Book of Common Prayer: A Spiritual Treasure Chest—
Selections Annotated & Explained
Annotation by The Rev. Canon C. K. Robertson, PhD; Foreword by The Most Rev. Katharine Jefferts Schori; Preface by Archbishop Desmond Tutu
Makes available the riches of this spiritual treasure chest for all who are interested in deepening their life of prayer, building stronger relationships and making a difference in their world. 5½ x 8½, 208 pp, Quality PB, 978-1-59473-524-0 **$16.99**

Celtic Christian Spirituality: Essential Writings—Annotated & Explained
Annotation by Mary C. Earle; Foreword by John Philip Newell
Explores how the writings of this lively tradition embody the gospel.
5½ x 8½, 176 pp, Quality PB, 978-1-59473-302-4 **$16.99**

Desert Fathers and Mothers: Early Christian Wisdom Sayings—
Annotated & Explained *Annotation by Christine Valters Paintner, PhD*
Opens up wisdom of the desert fathers and mothers for readers with no previous knowledge of Western monasticism and early Christianity.
5½ x 8½, 192 pp, Quality PB, 978-1-59473-373-4 **$16.99**

The End of Days: Essential Selections from Apocalyptic Texts—
Annotated & Explained *Annotation by Robert G. Clouse, PhD*
Helps you understand the complex Christian visions of the end of the world.
5½ x 8½, 224 pp, Quality PB, 978-1-59473-170-9 **$16.99**

The Hidden Gospel of Matthew: Annotated & Explained
Translation & Annotation by Ron Miller
Discover the words and events that have the strongest connection to the historical Jesus.
5½ x 8½, 272 pp, Quality PB, 978-1-59473-038-2 **$16.99**

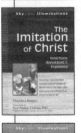

The Imitation of Christ: Selections Annotated & Explained
Annotation by Paul Wesley Chilcote, PhD; By Thomas à Kempis; Adapted from John Wesley's The Christian's Pattern
Let Jesus's example of holiness, humility and purity of heart be a companion on your own spiritual journey.
5½ x 8½, 224 pp, Quality PB, 978-1-59473-434-2 **$16.99**

The Infancy Gospels of Jesus: Apocryphal Tales from the Childhoods of Mary and Jesus—Annotated & Explained
Translation & Annotation by Stevan Davies; Foreword by A. Edward Siecienski, PhD
A startling presentation of the early lives of Mary, Jesus and other biblical figures that will amuse and surprise you. 5½ x 8½, 176 pp, Quality PB, 978-1-59473-258-4 **$16.99**

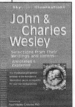

John & Charles Wesley: Selections from Their Writings and Hymns—
Annotated & Explained *Annotation by Paul W. Chilcote, PhD*
A unique presentation of the writings of these two inspiring brothers brings together some of the most essential material from their large corpus of work.
5½ x 8½, 288 pp, Quality PB, 978-1-59473-309-3 **$16.99**

Julian of Norwich: Selections from *Revelations of Divine Love*—
Annotated & Explained *Annotation by Mary C. Earle; Foreword by Roberta C. Bondi*
Addresses topics including the infinite nature of God, the life of prayer, God's suffering with us, the eternal and undying life of the soul, the motherhood of Jesus and the motherhood of God and more.
5½ x 8½, 224 pp, Quality PB, 978-1-59473-513-4 **$16.99**

Sacred Texts—continued

CHRISTIANITY—continued

The Lost Sayings of Jesus: Teachings from Ancient Christian, Jewish, Gnostic and Islamic Sources—Annotated & Explained
Translation & Annotation by Andrew Phillip Smith; Foreword by Stephan A. Hoeller
Depicts Jesus as a Wisdom teacher who speaks to people of all faiths as a mystic and spiritual master. 5½ x 8½, 240 pp, Quality PB, 978-1-59473-172-3 **$16.99**

Philokalia: The Eastern Christian Spiritual Texts—Selections Annotated & Explained *Annotation by Allyne Smith; Translation by G. E. H. Palmer, Phillip Sherrard and Bishop Kallistos Ware* The first approachable introduction to the wisdom of the Philokalia. 5½ x 8½, 240 pp, Quality PB, 978-1-59473-103-7 **$18.99**

The Sacred Writings of Paul: Selections Annotated & Explained
Translation & Annotation by Ron Miller Leads you into the exciting immediacy of Paul's teachings. 5½ x 8½, 224 pp, Quality PB, 978-1-59473-213-3 **$16.99**

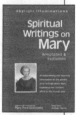

Saint Augustine of Hippo: Selections from *Confessions* and Other Essential Writings—Annotated & Explained
Annotation by Joseph T. Kelley, PhD; Translation by the Augustinian Heritage Institute
Provides insight into the mind and heart of this foundational Christian figure.
5½ x 8½, 272 pp, Quality PB, 978-1-59473-282-9 **$18.99**

Saint Ignatius Loyola—The Spiritual Writings: Selections Annotated & Explained *Annotation by Mark Mossa, SJ* Focuses on the practical mysticism of Ignatius of Loyola. 5½ x 8½, 288 pp, Quality PB, 978-1-59473-301-7 **$18.99**

Sex Texts from the Bible: Selections Annotated & Explained
Translation & Annotation by Teresa J. Hornsby; Foreword by Amy-Jill Levine
Demystifies the Bible's ideas on gender roles, marriage, sexual orientation, virginity, lust and sexual pleasure. 5½ x 8½, 208 pp, Quality PB, 978-1-59473-217-1 **$16.99**

Spiritual Writings on Mary: Annotated & Explained
Annotation by Mary Ford-Grabowsky; Foreword by Andrew Harvey
Examines the role of Mary, the mother of Jesus, as a source of inspiration in history and in life today. 5½ x 8½, 272 pp, Quality PB, 978-1-59473-001-6 **$16.99**

The Way of a Pilgrim: The Jesus Prayer Journey—Annotated & Explained
Translation & Annotation by Gleb Pokrovsky; Foreword by Andrew Harvey A classic of Russian Orthodox spirituality. 5¼ x 8½, 160 pp, Illus., Quality PB, 978-1-893361-31-7 **$15.99**

GNOSTICISM

Gnostic Writings on the Soul: Annotated & Explained
Translation & Annotation by Andrew Phillip Smith; Foreword by Stephan A. Hoeller
Reveals the inspiring ways your soul can remember and return to its unique, divine purpose. 5½ x 8½, 144 pp, Quality PB, 978-1-59473-220-1 **$16.99**

The Gospel of Philip: Annotated & Explained
Translation & Annotation by Andrew Phillip Smith; Foreword by Stevan Davies
Reveals otherwise unrecorded sayings of Jesus and fragments of Gnostic mythology.
5½ x 8½, 160 pp, Quality PB, 978-1-59473-111-2 **$16.99**

The Gospel of Thomas: Annotated & Explained
Translation & Annotation by Stevan Davies; Foreword by Andrew Harvey
Sheds new light on the origins of Christianity and portrays Jesus as a wisdom-loving sage.
5½ x 8½, 192 pp, Quality PB, 978-1-893361-45-4 **$16.99**

The Secret Book of John: The Gnostic Gospel—Annotated & Explained
Translation & Annotation by Stevan Davies The most significant and influential text of the ancient Gnostic religion. 5½ x 8½, 208 pp, Quality PB, 978-1-59473-082-5 **$18.99**

See Inspiration for *Perennial Wisdom for the Spiritually Independent: Sacred Teachings—Annotated & Explained*

Spirituality / Animal Companions

Blessing the Animals
Prayers and Ceremonies to Celebrate God's Creatures, Wild and Tame
Edited and with Introductions by Lynn L. Caruso
5 x 7¼, 256 pp, Quality PB, 978-1-59473-253-9 **$15.99**; HC, 978-1-59473-145-7 **$19.99**

Remembering My Pet
A Kid's Own Spiritual Workbook for When a Pet Dies
By Nechama Liss-Levinson, PhD, and Rev. Molly Phinney Baskette, MDiv
Foreword by Lynn L. Caruso
8 x 10, 48 pp, 2-color text, HC, 978-1-59473-221-8 **$16.99**

What Animals Can Teach Us about Spirituality
Inspiring Lessons from Wild and Tame Creatures
By Diana L. Guerrero 6 x 9, 176 pp, Quality PB, 978-1-893361-84-3 **$18.99**

Spirituality & Crafts

Beading—The Creative Spirit
Finding Your Sacred Center through the Art of Beadwork
By Rev. Wendy Ellsworth
Invites you on a spiritual pilgrimage into the kaleidoscope world of glass and color.
7 x 9, 240 pp, 8-page color insert, 40+ b/w photos and 40 diagrams
Quality PB, 978-1-59473-267-6 **$18.99**

Contemplative Crochet
A Hands-On Guide for Interlocking Faith and Craft
By Cindy Crandall-Frazier; Foreword by Linda Skolnik
Illuminates the spiritual lessons you can learn through crocheting.
7 x 9, 208 pp, b/w photos, Quality PB, 978-1-59473-238-6 **$16.99**

The Knitting Way
A Guide to Spiritual Self-Discovery
By Linda Skolnik and Janice MacDaniels
Examines how you can explore and strengthen your spiritual life through knitting.
7 x 9, 240 pp, b/w photos, Quality PB, 978-1-59473-079-5 **$16.99**

The Painting Path
Embodying Spiritual Discovery through Yoga, Brush and Color
By Linda Novick; Foreword by Richard Segalman
Explores the divine connection you can experience through art.
7 x 9, 208 pp, 8-page color insert, plus b/w photos, Quality PB, 978-1-59473-226-3 **$18.99**

The Quilting Path
A Guide to Spiritual Discovery through Fabric, Thread and Kabbalah
By Louise Silk
Explores how to cultivate personal growth through quilt making.
7 x 9, 192 pp, b/w photos and illus., Quality PB, 978-1-59473-206-5 **$16.99**

The Scrapbooking Journey
A Hands-On Guide to Spiritual Discovery
By Cory Richardson-Lauve; Foreword by Stacy Julian
Reveals how this craft can become a practice used to deepen and shape your life.
7 x 9, 176 pp, 8-page color insert, plus b/w photos, Quality PB, 978-1-59473-216-4 **$18.99**

The Soulwork of Clay
A Hands-On Approach to Spirituality
By Marjory Zoet Bankson; Photos by Peter Bankson
Takes you through the seven-step process of making clay into a pot, drawing
parallels at each stage to the process of spiritual growth.
7 x 9, 192 pp, b/w photos, Quality PB, 978-1-59473-249-2 **$16.99**

Spiritual Poetry—The Mystic Poets

Experience these mystic poets as you never have before. Each beautiful, compact book includes a brief introduction to the poet's time and place, a summary of the major themes of the poet's mysticism and religious tradition, essential selections from the poet's most important works, and an appreciative preface by a contemporary spiritual writer.

Hafiz
The Mystic Poets
Translated and with Notes by Gertrude Bell
Preface by Ibrahim Gamard

Hafiz is known throughout the world as Persia's greatest poet, with sales of his poems in Iran today only surpassed by those of the Qur'an itself. His probing and joyful verse speaks to people from all backgrounds who long to taste and feel divine love and experience harmony with all living things.

5 x 7¼, 144 pp, HC, 978-1-59473-009-2 **$16.99**

Hopkins
The Mystic Poets
Preface by Rev. Thomas Ryan, CSP

Gerard Manley Hopkins, Christian mystical poet, is beloved for his use of fresh language and startling metaphors to describe the world around him. Although his verse is lovely, beneath the surface lies a searching soul, wrestling with and yearning for God.

5 x 7¼, 112 pp, HC, 978-1-59473-010-8 **$16.99**

Tagore
The Mystic Poets
Preface by Swami Adiswarananda

Rabindranath Tagore is often considered the Shakespeare of modern India. A great mystic, Tagore was the teacher of W. B. Yeats and Robert Frost, the close friend of Albert Einstein and Mahatma Gandhi, and the winner of the Nobel Prize for Literature. This beautiful sampling of Tagore's two most important works, *The Gardener* and *Gitanjali,* offers a glimpse into his spiritual vision that has inspired people around the world.

5 x 7¼, 144 pp, HC, 978-1-59473-008-5 **$16.99**

Whitman
The Mystic Poets
Preface by Gary David Comstock

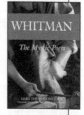

Walt Whitman was the most innovative and influential poet of the nineteenth century. This beautiful sampling of Whitman's most important poetry from *Leaves of Grass,* and selections from his prose writings, offers a glimpse into the spiritual side of his most radical themes—love for country, love for others and love of self.

5 x 7¼, 192 pp, HC, 978-1-59473-041-2 **$16.99**

Children's Spirituality

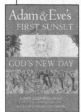

Adam & Eve's First Sunset: God's New Day
By Sandy Eisenberg Sasso; Full-color illus. by Joani Keller Rothenberg
A lesson in hope and faith—and that there are some things beyond our control—for every child who worries about what comes next.
9 x 12, 32 pp, Full-color illus., HC, 978-1-58023-177-0 **$17.95*** For ages 4 & up

Because Nothing Looks Like God
By Lawrence Kushner and Karen Kushner; Full-color illus. by Dawn W. Majewski
Invites parents and children to explore the questions we all have about God.
11 x 8½, 32 pp, Full-color illus., HC, 978-1-58023-092-6 **$18.99*** For ages 4 & up

Also Available: **Teacher's Guide** 8½ x 11, 22 pp, PB, 978-1-58023-140-4 **$6.95**

But God Remembered: Stories of Women from Creation to the Promised Land
By Sandy Eisenberg Sasso; Full-color illus. by Bethanne Andersen
A fascinating collection of four different stories of women only briefly mentioned in biblical tradition and religious texts.
9 x 12, 32 pp, Full-color illus., Quality PB, 978-1-58023-372-9 **$8.99*** For ages 8 & up

Does God Hear My Prayer?
By August Gold; Full-color photos by Diane Hardy Waller
Introduces preschoolers and young readers to prayer and how it helps them express their own emotions.
10 x 8½, 32 pp, Full-color photo illus., Quality PB, 978-1-59473-102-0 **$8.99** For ages 3–6

For Heaven's Sake *By Sandy Eisenberg Sasso; Full-color illus. by Kathryn Kunz Finney*
Heaven is often found where you least expect it.
9 x 12, 32 pp, Full-color illus., HC, 978-1-58023-054-4 **$16.95*** For ages 4 & up

In Our Image: God's First Creatures
By Nancy Sohn Swartz God asks all of nature to offer gifts to humankind—with a promise that the humans would care for creation in return.
Full-color illus., eBook, 978-1-58023-520-4 **$16.95*** For ages 5 & up
Animated app available on Apple App Store and The Google Play Marketplace **$9.99**

God's Paintbrush: Special 10th Anniversary Edition
By Sandy Eisenberg Sasso; Full-color illus. by Annette Compton
Invites children of all faiths and backgrounds to encounter God through moments in their own lives.
11 x 8½, 32 pp, Full-color illus., HC, 978-1-58023-195-4 **$17.95*** For ages 4 & up

Also Available: **God's Paintbrush Teacher's Guide**
8½ x 11, 32 pp, PB, 978-1-879045-57-6 **$8.95**

God's Paintbrush Celebration Kit: A Spiritual Activity Kit for Teachers and Students of All Faiths, All Backgrounds 9½ x 12, 40 Full-color Activity Sheets & Teacher Folder w/ complete instructions, HC, 978-1-58023-050-6 **$21.95**
Additional activity sheets available:
8-Student Activity Sheet Pack (40 sheets/5 sessions), 978-1-58023-058-2 **$19.95**
Single-Student Activity Sheet Pack (5 sessions), 978-1-58023-059-9 **$3.95**

Also Available as a Board Book: **I Am God's Paintbrush**
5 x 5, 24 pp, Full-color illus., Board Book, 978-1-59473-265-2 **$7.99** For ages 1–4

It's a … It's a … It's a Mitzvah
By Liz Suneby and Diane Heiman; Full-color Illus. by Laurel Molk
A whimsical, fun-filled book that helps parents and young children explore the joys of doing good deeds together.
9 x 12, 32 pp Full-color illus., HC, 978-1-58023-509-9 **$18.99*** For ages 3–6

Also Available as a Board Book: **That's a Mitzvah**
5 x 5, 24 pp, Full-color illus., Board Book, 978-1-58023-804-5 **$8.99*** For ages 1–4

*A book from Jewish Lights, SkyLight Paths' sister imprint

Children's Spirituality

Lullaby
By Debbie Friedman; Full-color illus. by Lorraine Bubar
A charming adaptation of beloved singer-songwriter Debbie Friedman's bestselling song *Lullaby*, this timeless bedtime picture book will help children know that God will keep them safe throughout the night.
9 x 12, 32 pp, Full-color illus. w/ a CD of original music & lyrics by Debbie Friedman
HC, 978-1-58023-807-6 **$18.99*** *For ages 3–6*

Remembering My Grandparent: A Kid's Own Grief Workbook in the Christian Tradition *By Nechama Liss-Levinson, PhD and Rev. Molly Phinney Baskette, MDiv*
8 x 10, 48 pp, 2-color text, HC, 978-1-59473-212-6 **$16.99** *For ages 7 & up*

Does God Ever Sleep? *By Joan Sauro, CSJ*
A charming nighttime reminder that God is always present in our lives.
10 x 8¼, 32 pp, Full-color photos, Quality PB, 978-1-59473-110-5 **$8.99** *For ages 3–6*

Does God Forgive Me? *By August Gold; Full-color photos by Diane Hardy Waller*
Gently shows how God forgives all that we do if we are truly sorry.
10 x 8¼, 32 pp, Full-color photos, Quality PB, 978-1-59473-142-6 **$8.99** *For ages 3–6*

God Said Amen *By Sandy Eisenberg Sasso; Full-color illus. by Avi Katz*
A warm and inspiring tale that shows us that we need only reach out to each other to find the answers to our prayers.
9 x 12, 32 pp, Full-color illus., HC, 978-1-58023-080-3 **$16.95*** *For ages 4 & up*

How Does God Listen? *By Kay Lindahl; Full-color photos by Cynthia Maloney*
How do we know when God is listening to us? Children will find the answers to these questions as they engage their senses while the story unfolds, learning how God listens in the wind, waves, clouds, hot chocolate, perfume, our tears and our laughter.
10 x 8¼, 32 pp, Full-color photos, Quality PB, 978-1-59473-084-9 **$8.99** *For ages 3–6*

In God's Hands *By Lawrence Kushner and Gary Schmidt; Full-color illus. by Matthew J. Baek*
A delightful, timeless legend that tells of the ordinary miracles that occur when we really, truly open our eyes to the world around us.
9 x 12, 32 pp, Full-color illus., HC, 978-1-58023-224-1 **$16.99*** *For ages 5 & up*

In God's Name *By Sandy Eisenberg Sasso; Full-color illus. by Phoebe Stone*
Like an ancient myth in its poetic text and vibrant illustrations, this award-winning modern fable about the search for God's name celebrates the diversity and, at the same time, the unity of all the people of the world.
9 x 12, 32 pp, Full-color illus., HC, 978-1-879045-26-2 **$18.99*** *For ages 4 & up*

Also Available in Spanish: El nombre de Dios
9 x 12, 32 pp, Full-color illus., HC, 978-1-893361-63-8 **$16.95**

Noah's Wife: The Story of Naamah
By Sandy Eisenberg Sasso; Full-color illus. by Bethanne Andersen
Opens young readers' religious imaginations to new ideas about the well-known story of the Flood. When God tells Noah to bring the animals of the world onto the ark, God also calls on Naamah, Noah's wife, to save each plant on Earth.
9 x 12, 32 pp, Full-color illus., HC, 978-1-58023-134-3 **$16.95*** *For ages 4 & up*

Also Available as a Board Book: Naamah, Noah's Wife
5 x 5, 24 pp, Full-color illus., Board Book, 978-1-893361-56-0 **$7.95** *For ages 1–4*

Where Does God Live? *By August Gold and Matthew J. Perlman*
Helps children and their parents find God in the world around us with simple, practical examples children can relate to.
10 x 8¼, 32 pp, Full-color photos, Quality PB, 978-1-893361-39-3 **$8.99** *For ages 3–6*

*A book from Jewish Lights, SkyLight Paths' sister imprint

Children's Spiritual Biography

MULTICULTURAL, NONDENOMINATIONAL, NONSECTARIAN

Ten Amazing People
And How They Changed the World
By Maura D. Shaw; Foreword by Dr. Robert Coles
Full-color illus. by Stephen Marchesi

For ages 7 & up

Shows kids that spiritual people can have an exciting impact on the world around them. Kids will delight in reading about these amazing people and what they accomplished through their words and actions.

Black Elk • Dorothy Day • Malcolm X • Mahatma Gandhi • Martin Luther King, Jr. • Mother Teresa • Janusz Korczak • Desmond Tutu • Thich Nhat Hanh • Albert Schweitzer

"Best Juvenile/Young Adult Non-Fiction Book of the Year."
—*Independent Publisher*

"Will inspire adults and children alike."
—*Globe and Mail* (Toronto)

8½ x 11, 48 pp, Full-color illus., HC, 978-1-893361-47-8 **$18.99** *For ages 7 & up*

Spiritual Biographies for Young People
For Ages 7 & Up

By Maura D. Shaw; Illus. by Stephen Marchesi
6¾ x 8¾, 32 pp, Full-color and b/w illus., HC

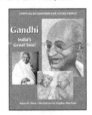
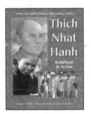

Black Elk: Native American Man of Spirit
Through historically accurate illustrations and photos, inspiring age-appropriate activities and Black Elk's own words, this colorful biography introduces children to a remarkable person who ensured that the traditions and beliefs of his people would not be forgotten.
978-1-59473-043-6 **$12.99**

Dorothy Day: A Catholic Life of Action
Introduces children to one of the most inspiring women of the twentieth century, a down-to-earth spiritual leader who saw the presence of God in every person she met. Includes practical activities, a timeline and a list of important words to know.
978-1-59473-011-5 **$12.99**

Gandhi: India's Great Soul
The only biography of Gandhi that balances a simple text with illustrations, photos and activities that encourage children and adults to talk about how to make changes happen without violence. Introduces children to important concepts of freedom, equality and justice among people of all backgrounds and religions.
978-1-893361-91-1 **$12.95**

Thich Nhat Hanh: Buddhism in Action
Warm illustrations, photos, age-appropriate activities and Thich Nhat Hanh's own poems introduce a great man to children in a way they can understand and enjoy. Includes a list of important Buddhist words to know.
978-1-893361-87-4 **$12.95**

Judaism / Christianity / Islam / Interfaith

Practical Interfaith: How to Find Our Common Humanity as We Celebrate Diversity
By Rev. Steven Greenebaum
Explores Interfaith as a faith—and as a positive way to move forward. Offers a practical, down-to-earth approach to a more spiritually fulfilling life.
6 x 9, 176 pp, Quality PB, 978-1-59473-569-1 **$16.99**

Sacred Laughter of the Sufis: Awakening the Soul with the Mulla's Comic Teaching Stories & Other Islamic Wisdom
By Imam Jamal Rahman
The legendary wisdom stories of the Mulla, Islam's great comic foil, with spiritual insights for seekers of all traditions—or none.
6 x 9, 192 pp, Quality PB, 978-1-59473-547-9 **$16.99**

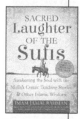

Spiritual Gems of Islam: Insights & Practices from the Qur'an, Hadith, Rumi & Muslim Teaching Stories to Enlighten the Heart & Mind
By Imam Jamal Rahman
Invites you—no matter what your practice may be—to access the treasure chest of Islamic spirituality and use its wealth in your own journey.
6 x 9, 256 pp, Quality PB, 978-1-59473-430-4 **$16.99**

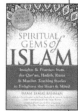

Religion Gone Astray: What We Found at the Heart of Interfaith
By Pastor Don Mackenzie, Rabbi Ted Falcon and Imam Jamal Rahman
Welcome to the deeper dimensions of interfaith dialogue—exploring that which divides us personally, spiritually and institutionally.
6 x 9, 192 pp, Quality PB, 978-1-59473-317-8 **$18.99**

Blessed Relief: What Christians Can Learn from Buddhists about Suffering
By Gordon Peerman 6 x 9, 208 pp, Quality PB, 978-1-59473-252-2 **$16.99**

Christians & Jews—Faith to Faith: Tragic History, Promising Present, Fragile Future *By Rabbi James Rudin*
6 x 9, 288 pp, HC, 978-1-58023-432-0 **$24.99**; Quality PB, 978-1-58023-717-8 **$18.99***

Christians & Jews in Dialogue: Learning in the Presence of the Other
By Mary C. Boys and Sara S. Lee; Foreword by Dorothy C. Bass
6 x 9, 240 pp, Quality PB, 978-1-59473-254-6 **$18.99**

Getting to the Heart of Interfaith: The Eye-Opening, Hope-Filled Friendship of a Pastor, a Rabbi & an Imam *By Pastor Don Mackenzie, Rabbi Ted Falcon and Imam Jamal Rahman*
6 x 9, 192 pp, Quality PB, 978-1-59473-263-8 **$16.99**

Hearing the Call across Traditions: Readings on Faith and Service
Edited by Adam Davis; Foreword by Eboo Patel
6 x 9, 352 pp, Quality PB, 978-1-59473-303-1 **$18.99**

InterActive Faith: The Essential Interreligious Community-Building Handbook
Edited by Rev. Bud Heckman with Rori Picker Neiss; Foreword by Rev. Dirk Ficca
6 x 9, 304 pp, Quality PB, 978-1-59473-273-7 **$16.99**; HC, 978-1-59473-237-9 **$29.99**

The Jewish Approach to God: A Brief Introduction for Christians
By Rabbi Neil Gillman, PhD 5½ x 8½, 192 pp, Quality PB, 978-1-58023-190-9 **$16.95***

The Jewish Approach to Repairing the World (Tikkun Olam)
A Brief Introduction for Christians *By Rabbi Elliot N. Dorff, PhD, with Rev. Cory Willson*
5½ x 8½, 256 pp, Quality PB, 978-1-58023-349-1 **$16.99***

The Jewish Connection to Israel, the Promised Land: A Brief Introduction for Christians *By Rabbi Eugene Korn, PhD* 5½ x 8½, 192 pp, Quality PB, 978-1-58023-318-7 **$14.99***

Jewish Holidays: A Brief Introduction for Christians *By Rabbi Kerry M. Olitzky and Rabbi Daniel Judson* 5½ x 8½, 176 pp, Quality PB, 978-1-58023-302-6 **$18.99***

Jewish Ritual: A Brief Introduction for Christians *By Rabbi Kerry M. Olitzky and Rabbi Daniel Judson* 5½ x 8½, 144 pp, Quality PB, 978-1-58023-210-4 **$14.99***

Jewish Spirituality: A Brief Introduction for Christians
By Rabbi Lawrence Kushner 5½ x 8½, 112 pp, Quality PB, 978-1-58023-150-3 **$12.95***

*A book from Jewish Lights, SkyLight Paths' sister imprint

Spirituality

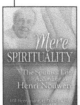

Mere Spirituality
The Spiritual Life According to Henri Nouwen
By Wil Hernandez, PhD, Obl. OSB; Foreword by Ronald Rolheiser
Introduction to Nouwen's spiritual thought, distills key insights on the realm of the spiritual life into one concise and compelling overview of his spirituality of the heart.
6 x 9, 160 pp (est), Quality PB, 978-1-59473-586-8 **$16.99**

The Forgiveness Handbook
Spiritual Wisdom and Practice for the Journey to Freedom, Healing and Peace
Created by the Editors at SkyLight Paths; Introduction by The Rev. Canon Marianne Wells Borg
Offers inspiration, encouragement and spiritual practice from across faith traditions for all who seek hope, wholeness and the freedom that comes from true forgiveness.
6 x 9, 256 pp, Quality PB, 978-1-59473-577-6 **$18.99**

Like a Child
Restoring the Awe, Wonder, Joy and Resiliency of the Human Spirit
By Rev. Timothy J. Mooney
By breaking free from our misperceptions about what it means to be an adult, we can reshape our world and become harbingers of grace. This unique spiritual resource explores Jesus's counsel to become like children in order to enter the kingdom of God. 6 x 9, 160 pp, Quality PB, 978-1-59473-543-1 **$16.99**

The Passionate Jesus: What We Can Learn from Jesus about Love, Fear, Grief, Joy and Living Authentically
By The Rev. Peter Wallace
Reveals Jesus as a passionate figure who was involved, present, connected, honest and direct with others and encourages you to build personal authenticity in every area of your own life. 6 x 9, 208 pp, Quality PB, 978-1-59473-393-2 **$18.99**

Gathering at God's Table: The Meaning of Mission in the Feast of Faith
By Katharine Jefferts Schori
A profound reminder of our role in the larger frame of God's dream for a restored and reconciled world. 6 x 9, 256 pp, HC, 978-1-59473-316-1 **$21.99**

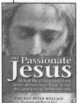

The Heartbeat of God: Finding the Sacred in the Middle of Everything
By Katharine Jefferts Schori; Foreword by Joan Chittister, OSB
Explores our connections to other people, to other nations and with the environment through the lens of faith.
6 x 9, 240 pp, HC, 978-1-59473-292-8 **$21.99**; Quality PB, 978-1-59473-589-9 **$16.99**

Laugh Your Way to Grace: Reclaiming the Spiritual Power of Humor
By Rev. Susan Sparks
A powerful, humorous case for laughter as a spiritual, healing path.
6 x 9, 176 pp, Quality PB, 978-1-59473-280-5 **$16.99**

Claiming Earth as Common Ground: The Ecological Crisis through the Lens of Faith
By Andrea Cohen-Kiener; Foreword by Rev. Sally Bingham
6 x 9, 192 pp, Quality PB, 978-1-59473-261-4 **$16.99**

Living into Hope: A Call to Spiritual Action for Such a Time as This
By Rev. Dr. Joan Brown Campbell; Foreword by Karen Armstrong
6 x 9, 208 pp, Quality PB, 978-1-59473-436-6 **$18.99**; HC, 978-1-59473-283-6 **$21.99**

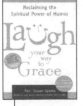

Renewal in the Wilderness
A Spiritual Guide to Connecting with God in the Natural World
By John Lionberger 6 x 9, 176 pp, b/w photos, Quality PB, 978-1-59473-219-5 **$16.99**

A Walk with Four Spiritual Guides: Krishna, Buddha, Jesus, and Ramakrishna
By Andrew Harvey 5½ x 8½, 192 pp, b/w photos & illus., Quality PB, 978-1-59473-138-9 **$18.99**

Spiritual Practice—The Sacred Art of Living Series

Teaching—The Sacred Art: The Joy of Opening Minds & Hearts
By Rev. Jane E. Vennard Explores the elements that make teaching a sacred art, recognizing it as a call to service rather than a job, and a vocation rather than a profession. 5½ x 8½, 160 pp, Quality PB, 978-1-59473-585-1 **$16.99**

Conversation—The Sacred Art: Practicing Presence in an Age of Distraction
By Diane M. Millis, PhD; Foreword by Rev. Tilden Edwards, PhD
5½ x 8½, 192 pp, Quality PB, 978-1-59473-474-8 **$16.99**

Dance—The Sacred Art: The Joy of Movement as a Spiritual Practice
By Cynthia Winton-Henry 5½ x 8½, 224 pp, Quality PB, 978-1-59473-268-3 **$16.99**

Dreaming—The Sacred Art: Incubating, Navigating & Interpreting Sacred Dreams for Spiritual & Personal Growth *By Lori Joan Swick, PhD*
5½ x 8½, 224 pp, Quality PB, 978-1-59473-544-8 **$16.99**

Fly-Fishing—The Sacred Art: Casting a Fly as a Spiritual Practice
By Rabbi Eric Eisenkramer and Rev. Michael Attas, MD; Foreword by Chris Wood, CEO, Trout Unlimited; Preface by Lori Simon, executive director, Casting for Recovery
5½ x 8½, 160 pp, Quality PB, 978-1-59473-299-7 **$16.99**

Giving—The Sacred Art: Creating a Lifestyle of Generosity
By Lauren Tyler Wright 5½ x 8½, 208 pp, Quality PB, 978-1-59473-224-9 **$16.99**

Haiku—The Sacred Art: A Spiritual Practice in Three Lines
By Margaret D. McGee 5½ x 8½, 192 pp, Quality PB, 978-1-59473-269-0 **$16.99**

Hospitality—The Sacred Art: Discovering the Hidden Spiritual Power of Invitation and Welcome *By Rev. Nanette Sawyer; Foreword by Rev. Dirk Ficca*
5½ x 8½, 208 pp, Quality PB, 978-1-59473-228-7 **$16.99**

Labyrinths from the Outside In, 2nd Edition
Walking to Spiritual Insight—A Beginner's Guide *By Rev. Dr. Donna Schaper and Rev. Dr. Carole Ann Camp* 6 x 9, 208 pp, b/w illus. and photos, Quality PB, 978-1-59473-486-1 **$16.99**

***Lectio Divina*—The Sacred Art**
Transforming Words & Images into Heart-Centered Prayer
By Christine Valters Paintner, PhD 5½ x 8½, 240 pp, Quality PB, 978-1-59473-300-0 **$16.99**

Pilgrimage—The Sacred Art: Journey to the Center of the Heart
By Dr. Sheryl A. Kujawa-Holbrook 5½ x 8½, 240 pp, Quality PB, 978-1-59473-472-4 **$16.99**

Practicing the Sacred Art of Listening
A Guide to Enrich Your Relationships and Kindle Your Spiritual Life
By Kay Lindahl 8 x 8, 176 pp, Quality PB, 978-1-893361-85-0 **$18.99**

Recovery—The Sacred Art: The Twelve Steps as Spiritual Practice *By Rami Shapiro*
Foreword by Joan Borysenko, PhD 5½ x 8½, 240 pp, Quality PB, 978-1-59473-259-1 **$16.99**

Running—The Sacred Art: Preparing to Practice *By Dr. Warren A. Kay*
Foreword by Kristin Armstrong 5½ x 8½, 160 pp, Quality PB, 978-1-59473-227-0 **$16.99**

The Sacred Art of Chant: Preparing to Practice
By Ana Hernández 5½ x 8½, 192 pp, Quality PB, 978-1-59473-036-8 **$16.99**

The Sacred Art of Fasting: Preparing to Practice
By Thomas Ryan, CSP 5½ x 8½, 192 pp, Quality PB, 978-1-59473-078-8 **$15.99**

The Sacred Art of Forgiveness: Forgiving Ourselves and Others through God's Grace
By Marcia Ford 8 x 8, 176 pp, Quality PB, 978-1-59473-175-4 **$18.99**

The Sacred Art of Listening: Forty Reflections for Cultivating a Spiritual Practice
By Kay Lindahl; Illus. by Amy Schnapper 8 x 8, 160 pp, b/w illus., Quality PB, 978-1-893361-44-7 **$16.99**

The Sacred Art of Lovingkindness: Preparing to Practice
By Rabbi Rami Shapiro; Foreword by Marcia Ford 5½ x 8½, 176 pp, Quality PB, 978-1-59473-151-8 **$16.99**

Spiritual Adventures in the Snow: Skiing & Snowboarding as Renewal for Your Soul
By Dr. Marcia McFee and Rev. Karen Foster; Foreword by Paul Arthur
5½ x 8½, 208 pp, Quality PB, 978-1-59473-270-6 **$16.99**

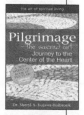

Thanking & Blessing—The Sacred Art: Spiritual Vitality through Gratefulness
By Jay Marshall, PhD; Foreword by Philip Gulley 5½ x 8½, 176 pp, Quality PB, 978-1-59473-231-7 **$16.99**

Writing—The Sacred Art: Beyond the Page to Spiritual Practice
By Rami Shapiro and Aaron Shapiro 5½ x 8½, 192 pp, Quality PB, 978-1-59473-372-7 **$16.99**

Retirement and Later-Life Spirituality

Caresharing
A Reciprocal Approach to Caregiving and Care Receiving in the Complexities of Aging, Illness or Disability
By Marty Richards
Shows how to move from independent to *inter*dependent caregiving, so that the "cared for" and the "carer" share a deep sense of connection.
6 x 9, 256 pp, Quality PB, 978-1-59473-286-7 **$16.99**; HC, 978-1-59473-247-8 **$24.99**

How Did I Get to Be 70 When I'm 35 Inside?
Spiritual Surprises of Later Life
By Linda Douty
Encourages you to focus on the inner changes of aging to help you greet your later years as the grand adventure they can be.
6 x 9, 208 pp, Quality PB, 978-1-59473-297-3 **$16.99**

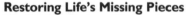

Soul Fire
Accessing Your Creativity
By Thomas Ryan, CSP
This inspiring guide shows you how to cultivate your creative spirit, particularly in the second half of life, as a way to encourage personal growth, enrich your spiritual life and deepen your communion with God.
6 x 9, 160 pp, Quality PB, 978-1-59473-243-0 **$16.99**

Restoring Life's Missing Pieces
The Spiritual Power of Remembering & Reuniting with People, Places, Things & Self
By Caren Goldman; Foreword by Dr. Nancy Copeland-Payton
Delve deeply into ways that your body, mind and spirit answer the Spirit of Re-union's calls to reconnect with people, places, things and self. A powerful and thought-provoking look at "reunions" of all kinds as roads to remembering the missing pieces of our stories, psyches and souls.
6 x 9, 208 pp, Quality PB, 978-1-59473-295-9 **$16.99**

Creative Aging
Rethinking Retirement and Non-Retirement in a Changing World
By Marjory Zoet Bankson
Explores the spiritual dimensions of retirement and aging and offers creative ways for you to share your gifts and experience, particularly when retirement leaves you questioning who you are when you are no longer defined by your career.
6 x 9, 160 pp, Quality PB, 978-1-59473-281-2 **$16.99**

Creating a Spiritual Retirement
A Guide to the Unseen Possibilities in Our Lives
By Molly Srode
Retirement can be an opportunity to refocus on your soul and deepen the presence of spirit in your life. With fresh spiritual reflections and questions to help you explore this new phase.
6 x 9, 208 pp, b/w photos, Quality PB, 978-1-59473-050-4 **$14.99**

Keeping Spiritual Balance as We Grow Older
More than 65 Creative Ways to Use Purpose, Prayer, and the Power of Spirit to Build a Meaningful Retirement
By Molly and Bernie Srode
As we face new demands on our bodies, it's easy to focus on the physical and forget about the transformations in our spiritual selves. This book is brimming with creative, practical ideas to add purpose and spirit to a meaningful retirement.
8 x 8, 224 pp, Quality PB, 978-1-59473-042-9 **$16.99**

Personal Growth

Deepening Engagement
Essential Wisdom for Listening and Leading with Purpose, Meaning and Joy
By Diane M. Millis, PhD; Foreword by Rob Lehman
A toolkit for community building as well as a resource for personal growth and small group enrichment.
5 x 7¼, 176 pp, Quality PB, 978-1-59473-584-4 **$14.99**

The Forgiveness Handbook
Spiritual Wisdom and Practice for the Journey to Freedom, Healing and Peace
Created by the Editors at SkyLight Paths; Introduction by The Rev. Canon Marianne Wells Borg
Offers inspiration, encouragement and spiritual practice from across faith traditions for all who seek hope, wholeness and the freedom that comes from true forgiveness. 6 x 9, 256 pp, Quality PB, 978-1-59473-577-6 **$18.99**

Decision Making & Spiritual Discernment: The Sacred Art of
Finding Your Way *By Nancy L. Bieber*
Presents three essential aspects of Spirit-led decision making: willingness, attentiveness and responsiveness.
5½ x 8½, 208 pp, Quality PB, 978-1-59473-289-8 **$16.99**

Like a Child
Restoring the Awe, Wonder, Joy and Resiliency of the Human Spirit
By Rev. Timothy J. Mooney
Explores Jesus's counsel to become like children in order to enter the kingdom of God. 6 x 9, 160 pp, Quality PB, 978-1-59473-543-1 **$16.99**

Secrets of a Soulful Marriage
Creating & Sustaining a Loving, Sacred Relationship
By Jim Sharon, EdD, and Ruth Sharon, MS
An innovative, hope-filled resource for developing soulful, mature love for committed couples who are looking to create, maintain and glorify the sacred in their relationship. Offers a banquet of practical tools, inspirational real-life stories and spiritual practices for couples of all faiths, or none.
6 x 9, 192 pp, Quality PB, 978-1-59473-554-7 **$16.99**

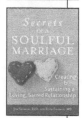

A Spirituality for Brokenness
Discovering Your Deepest Self in Difficult Times
By Terry Taylor
Compassionately guides you through the practicalities of facing and finally accepting brokenness in your life—a process that can ultimately bring mending.
6 x 9, 176 pp, Quality PB, 978-1-59473-229-4 **$16.99**

The Bridge to Forgiveness
Stories and Prayers for Finding God and Restoring Wholeness
By Karyn D. Kedar
6 x 9, 176 pp, Quality PB, 978-1-58023-451-1 **$16.99***

Conversation—The Sacred Art
Practicing Presence in an Age of Distraction
By Diane M. Millis, PhD; Foreword by Rev. Tilden Edwards, PhD
5½ x 8½, 192 pp, Quality PB, 978-1-59473-474-8 **$16.99**

Hospitality—The Sacred Art
Discovering the Hidden Spiritual Power of Invitation and Welcome
By Rev. Nanette Sawyer; Foreword by Rev. Dirk Ficca
5½ x 8½, 208 pp, Quality PB, 978-1-59473-228-7 **$16.99**

The Losses of Our Lives
The Sacred Gifts of Renewal in Everyday Loss
By Dr. Nancy Copeland-Payton
6 x 9, 192 pp, Quality PB, 978-1-59473-307-9 **$16.99**; HC, 978-1-59473-271-3 **$19.99**

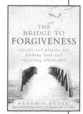

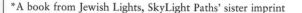

*A book from Jewish Lights, SkyLight Paths' sister imprint

Women's Interest

There's a Woman in the Pulpit: Christian Clergywomen Share Their Hard Days, Holy Moments & the Healing Power of Humor
Edited by Rev. Martha Spong; Foreword by Rev. Carol Howard Merritt
Offers insight into the lives of Christian clergywomen and the rigors that come with commitment to religious life, representing fourteen denominations as well as dozens of seminaries and colleges. 6 x 9, 240 pp, Quality PB, 978-1-59473-588-2 **$18.99**

She Lives! Sophia Wisdom Works in the World
By Rev. Jann Aldredge-Clanton, PhD
Fascinating narratives of clergy and laypeople who are changing the institutional church and society by restoring biblical female divine names and images to Christian theology, worship symbolism and liturgical language.
6 x 9, 320 pp, Quality PB, 978-1-59473-573-8 **$18.99**

Birthing God: Women's Experiences of the Divine
By Lana Dalberg; Foreword by Kathe Schaaf
Powerful narratives of suffering, love and hope that inspire both personal and collective transformation. 6 x 9, 304 pp, Quality PB, 978-1-59473-480-9 **$18.99**

Women, Spirituality and Transformative Leadership
Where Grace Meets Power
Edited by Kathe Schaaf, Kay Lindahl, Kathleen S. Hurty, PhD, and Reverend Guo Cheen
A dynamic conversation on the power of women's spiritual leadership and its emerging patterns of transformation.
6 x 9, 288 pp, Quality PB, 978-1-59473-548-6 **$18.99**; HC, 978-1-59473-313-0 **$24.99**

Spiritually Healthy Divorce: Navigating Disruption with Insight & Hope
By Carolyne Call A spiritual map to help you move through the twists and turns of divorce. 6 x 9, 224 pp, Quality PB, 978-1-59473-288-1 **$16.99**

Bread, Body, Spirit: Finding the Sacred in Food
Edited and with Introductions by Alice Peck 6 x 9, 224 pp, Quality PB, 978-1-59473-242-3 **$19.99**

Dance—The Sacred Art: The Joy of Movement as a Spiritual Practice
By Cynthia Winton-Henry 5½ x 8½, 224 pp, Quality PB, 978-1-59473-268-3 **$16.99**

Daughters of the Desert: Stories of Remarkable Women from Christian, Jewish and Muslim Traditions *By Claire Rudolf Murphy, Meghan Nuttall Sayres, Mary Cronk Farrell, Sarah Conover and Betsy Wharton*
5½ x 8½, 192 pp, Illus., Quality PB, 978-1-59473-106-8 **$16.99** Inc. reader's discussion guide

The Divine Feminine in Biblical Wisdom Literature
Selections Annotated & Explained
Translation & Annotation by Rabbi Rami Shapiro; Foreword by Rev. Cynthia Bourgeault, PhD
5½ x 8½, 240 pp, Quality PB, 978-1-59473-109-9 **$18.99**

Divining the Body: Reclaim the Holiness of Your Physical Self
By Jan Phillips 8 x 8, 256 pp, Quality PB, 978-1-59473-080-1 **$18.99**

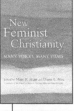

Honoring Motherhood: Prayers, Ceremonies & Blessings
Edited and with Introductions by Lynn L. Caruso
5 x 7¼, 272 pp, Quality PB, 978-1-58473-384-0 **$9.99**; HC, 978-1-59473-239-3 **$19.99**

New Feminist Christianity: Many Voices, Many Views
Edited by Mary E. Hunt and Diann L. Neu
6 x 9, 384 pp, Quality PB, 978-1-59473-435-9 **$19.99**; HC, 978-1-59473-285-0 **$24.99**

Next to Godliness: Finding the Sacred in Housekeeping
Edited by Alice Peck 6 x 9, 224 pp, Quality PB, 978-1-59473-214-0 **$19.99**

The Triumph of Eve & Other Subversive Bible Tales
By Matt Biers-Ariel 5½ x 8½, 192 pp, Quality PB, 978-1-59473-176-1 **$14.99**

Woman Spirit Awakening in Nature: Growing Into the Fullness of Who You Are
By Nancy Barrett Chickerneo, PhD; Foreword by Eileen Fisher
8 x 8, 224 pp, b/w illus., Quality PB, 978-1-59473-250-8 **$16.99**

Women of Color Pray: Voices of Strength, Faith, Healing, Hope and Courage
Edited and with Introductions by Christal M. Jackson 5 x 7¼, 208 pp, Quality PB, 978-1-59473-077-1 **$15.99**

Prayer / Meditation

Calling on God
Inclusive Christian Prayers for Three Years of Sundays
By Peter Bankson and Deborah Sokolove
Prayers for today's world, vividly written for Christians who long for a way to talk to and about God that feels fresh yet still connected to tradition.
6 x 9, 400 pp, Quality PB, 978-1-59473-568-4 **$18.99**

The Worship Leader's Guide to Calling on God
8½ x 11, 20 pp, PB, 978-1-59473-591-2 **$9.99**

Openings, 2nd Edition
A Daybook of Saints, Sages, Psalms and Prayer Practices
By Rev. Larry J. Peacock
For anyone hungry for a richer prayer life, this prayer book offers daily inspiration to help you move closer to God. Draws on a wide variety of resources—lives of saints and sages from every age, psalms, and suggestions for personal reflection and practice. 6 x 9, 448 pp, Quality PB, 978-1-59473-545-5 **$18.99**

Openings: A Daybook of Saints, Sages, Psalms and
Prayer Practices—Leader's Guide 8½ x 11, 12 pp, PB, 978-1-59473-572-1 **$9.99**

Men Pray: Voices of Strength, Faith, Healing, Hope and Courage
Created by the Editors at SkyLight Paths; With Introductions by Brian D. McLaren
Celebrates the rich variety of ways men around the world have called out to the Divine—with words of joy, praise, gratitude, wonder, petition and even anger—from the ancient world up to our own day.
5 x 7¼, 192 pp, HC, 978-1-59473-395-6 **$16.99**

Honest to God Prayer: Spirituality as Awareness, Empowerment,
Relinquishment and Paradox *By Kent Ira Groff*
6 x 9, 192 pp, Quality PB, 978-1-59473-433-5 **$16.99**

Lectio Divina—The Sacred Art
Transforming Words & Images into Heart-Centered Prayer
By Christine Valters Paintner, PhD
5½ x 8½, 240 pp, Quality PB, 978-1-59473-300-0 **$16.99**

Sacred Attention: A Spiritual Practice for Finding God in the Moment
By Margaret D. McGee 6 x 9, 144 pp, Quality PB, 978-1-59473-291-1 **$16.99**

Secrets of Prayer: A Multifaith Guide to Creating Personal Prayer in Your Life
By Nancy Corcoran, CSJ 6 x 9, 160 pp, Quality PB, 978-1-59473-215-7 **$16.99**

Women of Color Pray: Voices of Strength, Faith, Healing, Hope and Courage
Edited and with Introductions by Christal M. Jackson
5 x 7¼, 208 pp, Quality PB, 978-1-59473-077-1 **$15.99**

Prayer / M. Basil Pennington, OCSO

Finding Grace at the Center, 3rd Edition: The Beginning of
Centering Prayer *With Thomas Keating, OCSO, and Thomas E. Clarke, SJ*
Foreword by Rev. Cynthia Bourgeault, PhD A practical guide to a simple and beautiful form of meditative prayer. 5 x 7¼, 128 pp, Quality PB, 978-1-59473-182-2 **$12.99**

The Monks of Mount Athos: A Western Monk's Extraordinary
Spiritual Journey on Eastern Holy Ground *Foreword by Archimandrite Dionysios*
Explores the landscape, monastic communities and food of Athos.
6 x 9, 352 pp, Quality PB, 978-1-893361-78-2 **$18.95**

Psalms: A Spiritual Commentary *Illus. by Phillip Ratner*
Reflections on some of the most beloved passages from the Bible's most widely read book. 6 x 9, 176 pp, 24 full-page b/w illus., Quality PB, 978-1-59473-234-8 **$16.99**

The Song of Songs: A Spiritual Commentary *Illus. by Phillip Ratner*
Explore the Bible's most challenging mystical text.
6 x 9, 160 pp, 14 full-page b/w illus., Quality PB, 978-1-59473-235-5 **$16.99**
HC, 978-1-59473-004-7 **$19.99**

About SKYLIGHT PATHS Publishing

SkyLight Paths Publishing is creating a place where people of different spiritual traditions come together for challenge and inspiration, a place where we can help each other understand the mystery that lies at the heart of our existence.

Through spirituality, our religious beliefs are increasingly becoming a part of our lives—rather than *apart* from our lives. While many of us may be more interested than ever in spiritual growth, we may be less firmly planted in traditional religion. Yet, we do want to deepen our relationship to the sacred, to learn from our own as well as from other faith traditions, and to practice in new ways.

SkyLight Paths sees both believers and seekers as a community that increasingly transcends traditional boundaries of religion and denomination—people wanting to learn from each other, *walking together, finding the way.*

For your information and convenience, at the back of this book we have provided a list of other SkyLight Paths books you might find interesting and useful. They cover the following subjects:

Buddhism / Zen	Gnosticism	Poetry
Catholicism	Hinduism / Vedanta	Prayer
Chaplaincy		Religious Etiquette
Children's Books	Inspiration	Retirement & Later-Life Spirituality
Christianity	Islam / Sufism	
Comparative Religion	Judaism	Spiritual Biography
	Meditation	Spiritual Direction
Earth-Based Spirituality	Mindfulness	Spirituality
	Monasticism	Women's Interest
Enneagram	Mysticism	Worship
Global Spiritual Perspectives	Personal Growth	

Or phone, mail or email to: SKYLIGHT PATHS Publishing
An imprint of Turner Publishing Company
4507 Charlotte Avenue • Suite 100 • Nashville, Tennessee 37209
Tel: (615) 255-2665 • www.skylightpaths.com
Prices subject to change.

For more information about each book, visit our website at www.skylightpaths.com.

Printed in the USA
CPSIA information can be obtained
at www.ICGtesting.com
JSHW082338140824
68134JS00020B/1750

9 781594 733024